THE
GOLDEN
GRIMOIRE

THE
GOLDEN
GRIMOIRE

The Magical Way to
Wealth and Abundance

Dee
Norman

THE GOLDEN GRIMOIRE
Dee Norman

First published in the UK and USA in 2025 by
Watkins, an imprint of Watkins Media Limited
Unit 11, Shepperton House, 83–93 Shepperton Road
London N1 3DF

enquiries@watkinspublishing.com

A CIP record for this book is available from the British Library

ISBN: 978-1-78678-945-7 (Hardback)

ISBN: 978-1-78678-946-4 (eBook)

10 9 8 7 6 5 4 3 2 1

Printed and bound by
CPI Group (UK) Ltd, Croydon, CR0 4YY

Commissioning Editor: Ella Chappell
Managing Editor: Daniel Culver
Art Director: Karen Smith
Cover Design: Francesca Corsini
Interior Design and Typesetting: Alice Claire Coleman
Illustrations: Shutterstock
Production: Uzma Taj

www.watkinspublishing.com

To Brent, in thanks for going on
adventures and chasing dreams with me.

And to Selina. V'z tengrshy lbh'er
zl qnhtugre zber guna nalguvat.
– Ybir, (Ybh)Plcure.

CONTENTS

INTRODUCTION

A NOTE TO THE READER

A few of the spells in this book are based on information collected by a minister named Harry Middleton Hyatt. He was an amateur folklorist. Between 1936 and 1940 (and during some additional interviews he conducted in the 1970s), he collected over 13,000 folk magical practices and techniques from a myriad of African American hoodoo and rootwork practitioners throughout the southeastern United States. These spells were collected in a massive five-volume set called *Hoodoo-Conjuration-Witchcraft-Rootwork*.

Hyatt's work was Herculean, and I admire his dedication to recording these practices, many of which may have been lost without his efforts. However, I am more indebted to his informants, who were willing to open up and share information about some of their most private practices.

When I began writing this book, I debated about including spells drawn from Hyatt's work. But I have used these spells to great success, and they have brought me comfort over the years. I ask that if you use these spells, you remember their true source and handle them with reverence. I also hope you feel the same amount of gratitude toward the culture that developed them as I do.

Each spell derived from information from Hyatt's informants will be marked with a

A BLESSING

May anyone who touches this book be blessed with perpetual prosperity that fulfils their needs and provides them with the kinds of wealth they need to be successful, happy and spiritually satisfied. May all their financial difficulties melt away, resolving in the best possible way so the reader can continue their life unimpeded and content. May their anxieties ease, their worries vanish, and may they be blessed with the knowledge that they and their loved ones will be nurtured, and their needs will be met.

INTRODUCTION

Welcome to *The Golden Grimoire*! It is my sincere wish that this book will help you improve your present situation and establish a sound financial future.

Using magic and spiritual practices to improve your financial situation and increase your wealth is a topic that is extremely important to me, because it has helped me make significant changes which have allowed me to live the life I want to live. The road has not always been smooth, and the results have not always been direct, but magic combined with physical world work has helped me over the rough spots.

When I was growing up, my parents only ever seemed to get seriously upset about two things: the health and wellbeing of us kids, and money. Money was a constant topic of concern because we didn't have a lot of it.

More than anything, my folks wanted to give their kids more than what they'd had growing up. They believed that providing us with a good education was the key to our future successes.

My family is Italian American. When my grandfather first started attending school, he only spoke Italian. He was placed in a Spanish-speaking classroom because the school didn't provide instruction in his native language. My grandfather only went to school until sixth grade. I don't know how much education my grandmother had, but she could read and write, unlike her mother, who signed her greeting cards to the family with an X. My mother and her brother were sent to public schools, and both received a decent education.

But my family wanted more for us. They wanted to send us to private schools that would give us the type of education that they hoped would ensure greater opportunities. We were part of the great immigrant dream. Each generation must have a better chance at success than the previous one.

But private schools were an expense my family couldn't really afford. Especially with two children. That didn't stop my folks.

Throughout my life, I can remember times when my dad worked three jobs. Other times, he worked two and mowed grass on the weekends.

He did every kind of work you can imagine. At times he was a designing draughtsman, and he did a stint as a stockbroker. But he also worked at liquor stores, gas stations and fast-food restaurants. At one point, he taught math at a community college. Another time, he managed a miniature golf course and arcade. (As you can imagine, the summer he spent working here was my favourite. All the free tokens I could use, and my folks threw my birthday party there that year.)

My mother was a stay-at-home mom while we were growing up. While my brother and I were in school, she spent some time working with a friend of hers doing painting and wallpapering jobs. I was the youngest, and the moment I was old enough, she got a job and I got to live out my tweens as a latchkey kid. It gave her the freedom to work at card and gift stores.

My parents worked hard, and my grandparents helped them scrape by. And they did. And my brother and I got the education my folks dreamed of: private grade school and high school. My brother even went to a private university. I opted for a state university. And then we set out to make our ways in the world.

It's not always easy to get started, and I struggled with money. Luckily for me, my family didn't just instil in me a powerful work ethic that taught me to value working hard and saving money. I also had the immense blessing of growing up with an Italian American magical tradition, which opened my eyes to the power of magic early in my life.

With the encouragement of my mother and grandmother, I explored various styles of magic throughout my life. And I found my calling: studying all things esoteric and magical. When I started to live on my own, I naturally turned to magic to solve some of the financial difficulties I faced.

So this book contains the tried-and-tested methods I have used over the years throughout my financial journey. These spells are the ones that have worked for me, family and friends time and time again.

It is my sincere hope that *The Golden Grimoire* will help you achieve all your dreams.

WHAT THIS BOOK CAN DO

This book isn't a mundane guide about how to manage your money. There are plenty of books about that. *The Golden Grimoire* is here to provide you with a magical means to support your physical world efforts to improve your financial situation. You won't find advice about where to invest your money in these pages. And you won't find suggestions about how you can save mountains of money each year by giving up beloved habits like drinking expensive coffee.

What you will find here are magical and spiritual tools designed to meet you wherever you are on your financial journey and help you progress toward your goals. The spells and techniques I have included in this book are here because they work. I know they do, because I've experimented with all of them at different phases of my life.

My first experience with wealth magic happened by accident in my early twenties. I was strapped for cash and working a job that stressed me out and just about allowed me to scrape by. My debts were high, and I had no idea how I was going to pay them. One day, a coworker of mine admired a simple haematite ring I was wearing. I loved it even though it was a cheap ring I'd picked up at a tourist trap several years before. I knew she was going through some difficult times and could use a little protection, which haematite is good for. Impulsively, I offered her the ring. She didn't want to take it at first, but I emphasized that it was a trinket I'd picked up on a lark, that it brought me a lot of joy, and that maybe it might bring her some, too. She reluctantly took it. Soon after, her luck turned for the better. That simple act of low-level generosity initiated a series of fortunate events in my life. For the next two weeks, money fell in my lap! The experience taught me that stepping outside my own worries and acting for the good of others can turn my luck. It showed me that even when I don't have money, being generous with what I do have can be a magical act in itself. And it got me thinking about different magical and spiritual ways I could welcome wealth into my life.

I have worked fast and desperate spells because I didn't have enough money to pay my rent. I've healed my wealth wounds so I could feel comfortable enough to embark on a creative career of writing, art and magic. I have worked complex wealth spells to help maintain and enhance my financial state.

The path to wealth isn't linear, so I've turned to these spells over and over again throughout my life to bolster my confidence, smooth the way before me, and bring me the opportunities I need to get where I want to go.

If you are new to magic, I'd like to assure you that all the information you need to work the spells in this book is included. More excitingly, I hope this book will give you enough information so you can eventually create spells specific to your needs. If you've been around the block a few times, you know what parts to skip. Or you could read those parts anyway, and then tell me what I got wrong!

SECTION 1: SETTING THE SCENE

You will often hear that money spells are more difficult to work than other types of magic. In some ways, I agree. In the first section of this book, "Setting the Scene", I talk about why some folks struggle to use magic to attain wealth. Throughout the first section, we will discuss the things that can disrupt your magic, particularly when it comes to using it to fix your finances. We will also talk about wealth wounds – the mental, emotional and spiritual injuries we sustain that can prevent us from leading wealthy and fulfilled lives.

Of course, we are also going to talk about how to heal those wounds, avoid the common pitfalls that assail people when they attempt to embrace prosperity through magic, and find the right magical path to get you where you want to go.

The first section ends with a guide to assessing your current financial situation and acknowledging where you are today, without falling into a pit of despair or putting your aspirations away out of complacency.

SECTION 2: FOUNDATIONS OF FINANCIAL MAGIC

The second section of this book, "Foundations of Financial Magic", covers the following:

- How to read tarot cards to reveal your financial future, including complete interpretations specific to money and finances for each card, upright and reversed.
- How to create a personal prosperity sigil, which can be used by itself or in conjunction with the other spells in this book.
- How to build a wealth altar.
- How to use colours, gems and herbs to enhance your wealth magic.

SECTION 3: THE GOLDEN GRIMOIRE

Finally, the third section of this book is the grimoire proper. It contains all the spells, and is broken up into five parts.

Part I – Spiritual Allies

A short list of non-physical entities you may be interested in working with while conducting your magic. There are many different entities you may wish to include, from ancestors and spirits of a place, to saints, to god and goddess forms. This list is meant to kickstart your explorations and is by no means complete.

Part II – Money Spells

Spells that require a few common items, most of which you probably already have in your home. These spells are simple and direct. They focus on obtaining small sums of money quickly and stabilizing difficult financial situations.

Part III – Prosperity Spells

Spells that focus on improving your finances when they are in a stable state. They may require one or two specialty items or a few more components.

Part IV – Wealth Spells

Spells that are designed to maintain and sustain your wealth. You might choose to work these spells to enhance your overall wealth or support a business endeavour. These magical workings require the greatest number of materials.

Part V – Group Work

Information about working with groups, both in person and virtually. This section also includes information about how to design your own group rituals.

As you can see from the summary above, I've attempted to split the spells into groupings that apply to various points in your financial journey. However, you don't have to work through the spells (or this book) in order! I can't know your personal situation, and you will best understand which spells you need at which times. So pick and choose your spells as you see fit.

You should work through this book in the order you are most comfortable with, but I strongly suggest you read "Starting from Zero: Identifying and Healing Wealth Wounds" (page 38) and "Crafting a Personal Prosperity Sigil" (page 110) early in your exploration of financial magic. Armed with that information, you will be well equipped to manifest the prosperous and wealthy lifestyle of your dreams.

SETTING THE SCENE

WHAT ARE WE REALLY TALKING ABOUT AND WHY?

This part of *The Golden Grimoire* is here to arm you with knowledge you can use to make smart choices about establishing financial goals and setting your magical intentions. These are the building blocks to understanding yourself, where you currently are financially, and where you want to go. When you understand these things, you will be able to make informed, strategic decisions about financial matters that comply with both your plans for your future and your spiritual convictions.

Just the simple alignment between your spiritual and financial goals will do a great deal for your financial prospects – because if you are not of one mind about how you wish to manifest your future, you create unnecessary resistance for yourself.

DEFINING TERMS: MONEY, WEALTH AND PROSPERITY

Before we can talk about money, wealth and prosperity magic, we need to understand exactly what those words mean. These three words are often used interchangeably, but when you closely examine the definition of each, you will see that their distinct meanings help to illustrate a roadmap to financial fulfilment.

- The word **money** comes from the Latin word *moneta*. That word was actually part of the name of a Roman goddess: Juno Moneta. Her temple housed the Roman mint, where coins were made. Money is a medium of exchange widely accepted as a way to pay for goods and services. It is a way to store value. To give a simple example, you might trade your labour for money and then trade that money to pay for electricity or groceries. In modern times, the concept of money is often used to indicate things like property and other resources, but those are really assets. Money, whether physical or digital, is a specific item you own.

- The word **prosperity** comes from the Latin word *prosperitas* and originally meant good fortune and success. Breaking down the word into its component parts, we see that *pro* means forward and *spere* means hope. Prosperity thus literally means "moving forward with hope or good fortune". Eventually, in addition to indicating favourable conditions, the word began to include ideas about health and flourishing on all levels. Prosperity is a state of being.

- The word **wealth** comes from the Old English word *wela* and originally meant wellbeing and riches. When the word entered Middle English, the definition expanded to include possessions and assets. In modern English, the word has expanded even further, meaning an abundance of valuable resources of all kinds: possessions, wellbeing and even social status. Wealth is a mode of existence.

As a mode of existence, it is important to remember that wealth encompasses many more things than just the money in your bank account, the house you live in and the car you drive. Everyone values things differently, and it is important that you decide what constitutes wealth for you, in the context of your lifestyle.

Why am I picking these three words apart? Because deeply understanding them will help you focus on what kind of result you really want from the magic you practise. Do you want a small sum of cash? Do you want to perpetuate a state of being in which you have a lot of opportunities to grow and succeed? Or do you want to exist in a state in which all your needs are met, you have plenty of the resources *you* deem most valuable, and you maintain a sense of wellbeing?

Ultimately, we want all those things. But individual spells work toward specific goals, and understanding those goals will help to get you where you want to go.

Also, the deeper meanings of these words illustrate a logical progression. *Money* brings you the stability to sustain yourself and your household, opening you up to all the possibilities of *prosperity*. The opportunities encouraged by living in a prosperous state eventually bring you to *wealth*. That is why this book is subtitled *A Witch's Way to Wealth*. My goal is to help you start wherever you are, and magically support your efforts to move down the path toward the wealth and fulfilment of your dreams.

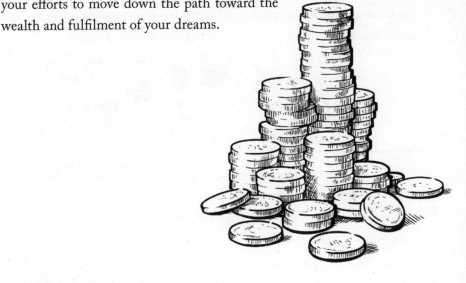

SETTING THE SCENE

MONEY, WEALTH AND PROSPERITY MAGIC

A definition of magic

Before talking about money, wealth and prosperity magic, let's pause and talk about what magic is. There has been a lot of ink spilled (some by me, even) in attempts to define magic. You may have already heard or read the definition Aleister Crowley (English magician, 1875–1947) included in his book *Magick in Theory and Practice*: "the Science and Art of causing Change to occur in conformity with Will".[1]

You will find as you read through this book that understanding yourself and your situation is critical when it comes to figuring out what you want to accomplish with your magic. You must achieve this first before you can apply that information and gain the results you desire.

You might be asking where the mysterious mystical part of the definition is. Crowley's explanation is broad and purposely includes nearly everything from getting out of bed in the morning to conducting a complex magical ritual.

For our purposes, let's define magic as the ability to effect change without visible/physical means, after fully understanding yourself and your situation.

---

1   But Crowley described magic in another way in his book, one that is particularly helpful when we consider wealth magic. He says that magic "is the science of understanding oneself and one's condition. It is the art of applying that understanding in action."

Money magic

Money magic is what it sounds like: magic targeted toward attaining money. Depending on how well the spell is constructed, it might bring you a specific amount of money or any amount at all. It is financial magic at its most basic. You ask the universe to provide you with cash and that's the end of the story. This approach isn't always the most effective. We will discuss why in "Money Magic Mysteries Revealed" (page 25). By the way, I don't hate money spells! There's a whole section stuffed with money spells in the third part of this book. However, they aren't always the perfect fit for every circumstance. Money magic is reactive. That means it usually responds to an existing situation or need.

Prosperity magic

Prosperity magic includes spells that open you up to new opportunities like better pay, better employment or more chances to generate wealth. I like to think of these spells as the momentum-makers. They are the ones that propel you into a future in which you will be wealthier and happier. They help smooth out the rough edges and make sure you don't hit any snags along the way as you work toward your goals. Prosperity magic can be reactive or proactive, depending on the situation. Proactive spells anticipate events and make changes so that things unfold as you desire.

Wealth magic

There is no "end of the road" when it comes to managing your wealth and finances. You are never done, at least as long as you are breathing. Wealth magic focuses on expanding and developing what you already have. It helps you protect yourself and your household, as you are in an enviable state. It also helps you seek out people who can help you plan for your future and consolidate your stability. Wealth magic is primarily proactive. It maintains your current state and helps you make plans for what comes next.

Reactive and proactive magic

Just a final word on reactive and proactive magic. Neither one is better than the other. In your day-to-day life and on your journey to wealth, you will experience many different situations. Some will happen out of the blue and require reactive magic. Others you will be able to plan for or work toward, and they will require proactive magic.

The more stable your financial situation becomes, the more you will perform less reactive magic, because you won't need to respond to emergency situations. However, a surprise popping up does not mean that your entire journey has gone off the rails. The spells in this book, reactive or proactive, are there to be used when you need them.

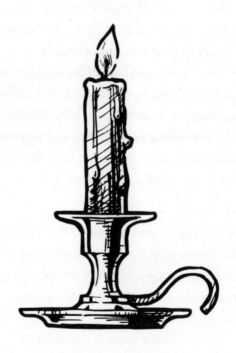

MONEY MAGIC
MYSTERIES REVEALED

As mentioned above, some people believe it is more difficult to successfully perform money magic than other sorts of magic. I spent a lot of time talking about this topic while I was researching and writing this book, and I received mixed reactions from people when they discovered what I was working on. Some folks were eager to read what I came up with, because they wanted to use magic to improve their financial situations but weren't sure how to go about it. Others were convinced that wealth magic was too difficult and dangerous to approach. Some were afraid it could backfire and result in financial ruin. And some were fearful that the performance of money magic could have other dire results that wouldn't be worth the financial benefits.

In my experience, money magic is no more difficult or dangerous than any other type. The trick is that it requires the same *attitude* and *approach* as other styles of magic. I believe that is where people struggle. There are specific challenges involved in financial magic that make it more difficult to maintain the right attitude and take the correct approach. In this section, we will examine these difficulties and how they can create barriers between you and your goals.

These issues break down into two general categories:

- ◊ Technical missteps that can be corrected by proper planning and execution of your spells and rituals
- ◊ Emotional/spiritual issues that can be resolved through gaining a deeper understanding of your beliefs and working through conflicts related to money and wealth

WHY DOES MONEY/WEALTH MAGIC SEEM TO FAIL MORE OFTEN THAN OTHER TYPES?

More than once, I have had friends come to me with the complaint that though they experience great success with other types of magic, obtaining their financial goals through magical means completely eludes them. These are folks who are experienced magicians and witches, who have talked themselves into the idea that money magic "just doesn't work for them".

Why do you think that is? I'll accept the fact that we all have different affinities and preferences for the types and styles of magic we practise, but I draw the line at thinking certain types of magic are only available to a select few.

Unfortunately, there is a tendency to talk ourselves into failure, especially if we have experienced one before. You are much less likely to work successful wealth magic if you approach it thinking, "Oh, I'll try this, but I'm *never any good* at money magic."

If you happen to feel that way, it's not the end of your career as a wealth witch. To rectify the situation, you must examine your core beliefs about money and wealth and resolve any issues you may have (*see* "Emotional/ Spiritual Barriers" on page 31).

HOW TO AVOID TECHNICAL MISSTEPS

Successful magic is a true fusion of fluidity and precision. You must plan carefully either via research or intuition, and then execute the spell with abandon and strong emotions. Most of the technical mishaps that take place have nothing to do with the execution of a spell. They aren't related to things like your concentration breaking for a split second or stumbling over a word. Instead, they stem from how well you understand what you are doing and the decisions you made while planning your spell. Here are some aspects that are important to focus on when you are planning your wealth magic (and all magic, in fact).

Be precise about your goals and intentions

Vague goals get vague results. To get the most out of your magic, you need a clearly defined goal that you can easily picture. The more concrete the better. If you want enough money to pay rent this month, that's a great goal. You can picture yourself writing the cheque or paying your rent online. If you want to find a new job, you can envision yourself receiving an acceptance email and employment package.

It's much harder to picture things like having enough money. Or not being in debt. These goals are more difficult to turn into concrete scenarios. That doesn't make these things impossible to achieve with magic. It just means you must work to ensure you can picture something specific that symbolizes those states. You need to dedicate some time to figuring out what having enough money means to you. This requires figuring out what kind of lifestyle you want to lead and learning how to picture it as vividly as possible. "Setting Your Intentions: Mindful Budgeting and Financial Planning" (page 62) can help you with this process.

Carefully word your goals and intentions

In addition to being able to visualize your goal, you must be able to state it simply and clearly. This helps you to hold that goal firmly in your mind while you are performing your magical work. It is part of the effort you must put into your spells to make them a success. Sometimes, when we find a spell in a book, the name of the spell gives us an idea of what our goal should be. If a spell is called the "Fast Cash Spell", you generally know the objective. But even in cases where the goal seems clear, make sure to personalize it. Though you do need to give the universe enough room to work on your behalf (*see* the next section), you also need to make the goals specific to your needs.

Goals that aren't stated in the present tense might delay your accomplishments, so be sure to word your goals appropriately. Though some folks recommend starting your goals with the words "I will" or "I wish", I prefer to construct my goal statements as though I already have what I am seeking. For example, if I want to work a spell to bring me enough money to start a side business, I would phrase it like this: "I have enough money to start my business." (Rather than "I will get enough money to start my business.") Your subconscious, which is one of your biggest magical allies, works best with the present tense.

And finally, do not state your goals in a negative way. For example, don't choose a goal like "I don't have any debt" or "I never run out of money". Don't insert another layer of meaning to wade through when you are working with your goal. Don't force your subconscious to deal with a negative concept. State your goals positively. "My debts disappear" or "I have plenty of money" will be easier to work with and will ensure better results.

Give the universe room to work

This is a tough one, especially after we just spent the previous two sections talking about precision. But this concept is important, especially when you are judging the efficacy of your magic. Magic is not linear and can work in unexpected ways.

Don't try to force the outcome of your spells to manifest in specific forms. The universe, your guides and spiritual allies, and the world at large are aware of many more options than you are, even if you are super-psychic or consult your oracle cards daily. When you work magic, you are giving the unseen forces permission to tinker with your fate to your benefit and the benefit of others. So don't try to corner them into doing things your way.

I had a friend, let's call them P, who wanted to make more money. They liked their job, but it was a struggle to make ends meet. So they did a spell to earn more money through their job. They expected to get a raise or a promotion (a logical expectation). But magic doesn't always work logically. What happened is that they got fired almost immediately. They lost their comfortable job. There was sadness and woe. The magic obviously backfired. They were worse off than when they began.

Except . . . three days after they lost their job, an old friend contacted P. It seemed there was an opening at the friend's company that needed to be filled right away. And it paid nearly a third more than what P had been making at their old job. P took the new job and had plenty of cash.

Later on, when I talked to P about the experience, they admitted that they never would have left their original job without giving at least two weeks' notice. They would have felt obligated to stay, and probably would have missed out on the opportunity to work with a friend doing something they loved and making the amount of money they were now making.

Once you work a spell, you must be willing to let go and allow the magic to manifest how it will, otherwise you could easily sabotage the outcome. It is difficult to let go and trust, but it gets easier the more magic you do. You get comfortable with knowing that things will just turn out right.

Do the physical, material world work

Magic can do anything! This is absolutely true. I believe it because I have seen amazing and marvellous things happen. I've experienced outcomes I never thought possible. Thanks to magic, stunning opportunities have fallen into my lap when I least expected it. I count the fact that I am writing this book one of them.

However, it is important to balance your magical work with, for lack of a better term, physical world work. (I sometimes say mundane work, but I don't really think any work is mundane work. I believe magic is interwoven throughout our entire lives.)

What do I mean by balancing magical and physical world work? Let's look at working magic to get a new job as an example. When I work a spell to get a new job, I can do one of two things when I am finished. On one hand, I can network with people who can help me discover job opportunities, I can search job boards, and I can apply for jobs that appeal to me. On the other hand, I can sit around my house waiting patiently for a job to literally magically appear. Guess which approach is more likely to succeed? I know it sounds overly simplistic, but this goes along with giving the universe enough elbow room to give you what you want. You have to shake things up a little bit by going out into the world and making yourself available. This increases the probability of success.

Yes, you can sit in your room impatiently working magic to get that new job, stubbornly refusing to do anything else. But even if it does work (which it may not, because you are contradicting your intent by not doing anything to help make it a reality), it will take much longer than if you just get out there and do the physical world work.

This generally isn't a problem for me, because if I feel motivated enough to work magic to accomplish something, it is a goal that I want so badly I am willing to do a lot of work, spiritually and physically, to attain it. But it often amazes me when I see people actively working against their magical intentions by not giving them as many chances as possible to come to fruition. So don't work against yourself by not getting active and doing what you can in the physical world to achieve your goals!

EMOTIONAL/SPIRITUAL BARRIERS

Though the technical issues listed in the section above can thwart your efforts, it is the issues in this section that spawn the most problems when attempting to work magic for prosperity and wealth. In other words, this stuff is important.

Emotional and spiritual issues surrounding money are the biggest barriers to a wealthy and satisfied life. Resolving those issues (which I call wealth wounds) increases your chances of magical success.

If any of the descriptions below sound familiar to you, check out "Starting from Zero: Identifying and Healing Wealth Wounds" on page 38.

Conflicting messages

What is your opinion of money? Oh, that's nice. But what is your *real, deep-down* opinion about money? I ask you this not to challenge you, but to point out the fact that throughout our lives, we are told many different conflicting things about the topic.

Sometimes, you'll hear that money is the root of all evil (though that is a common misquote; 1 Timothy 6:10 really reads "for the *love* of money is the root of all evil").

You also hear that it is a necessary evil, that it pays the piper, and that it makes the world go round. The movie *Wall Street* tells us "Greed is good", while we also hear that it can't buy happiness.

Do you think modern culture is a little bit conflicted about money and the role it plays in society? Is it any wonder that we are?

If you really want to dig deep, what's your opinion of capitalism? Are you comfortable with the idea of ownership of property?

On your path to wealth, one of the things you must do is come to terms with what wealth means *for you*. Does it simply mean money, or does it mean something more? Because wealth can represent an opulent lifestyle, but it can also mean living frugally to save for the future. One person may value their time over money, while another may value health over everything.

And no matter what, when coming to terms with your understanding of wealth, you have to decide what you think about money. Pursuing cold, hard cash won't do you any good if you truly agree that money is the root of all evil and all you really want is time to do the things you love. If that is indeed your picture of wealth, you will need to shape your intentions to support that. Meanwhile, if you think greed is good and you want a fancy penthouse with a view and a collection of classic cars, the intentions you set must match what you envision.

There is no judgement here and you don't have to confess your true feelings to anyone. They belong to you and you alone. But thinking about these topics and figuring out how you feel is another step on the way to preparing yourself for working powerful wealth magic.

Feelings of lack or limitation

Unlike magic for some other purposes, we often find ourselves turning to financial magic when we are faced with difficult real-world obstacles to our health and wellbeing.

If you are doing magic to increase your intuition or psychic abilities, the goal is a little bit more amorphous than if you are doing magic to help get enough money to put food on the table and avoid homelessness. There are times when lack of money poses an existential threat to you and your loved ones. Its absence is concrete and felt on all levels and in all aspects of your life.

When you are working against deep feelings of concern combined with feelings of lack, it can be difficult to put yourself into the positive, powerful mindset that is needed for magic. Feelings of doubt, insufficiency and failure start to creep in before you even get started. Questions and doubts can interfere with how completely you throw yourself into your magical work.

If your sense of lack is strong enough, you may find yourself haunted by an inability to focus on your goals or to fully envision them.

It is important to develop coping mechanisms and acknowledge the abundance around you so you can best prepare yourself for magical success.

To overcome these feelings, it helps to start with spells that focus on smaller, more specific goals. Once you experience a few successes, your confidence will build and you will be able to approach more complex intentions.

Fear of results

People unfamiliar with practical magic often approach the idea with more than a little trepidation or even fear. "What if my magic causes something terrible to happen?" they ask. When I start asking them about what they are afraid of, it turns out they are usually fearing some sort of monkey-paw experience in which they work magic for a seemingly innocent intent and yet end up cowering in their cottage while the desiccated corpse of their child scratches at the door.

Really, people can't be blamed for these fears.

There are many stories in folklore, literature and popular culture about magic going awry. Willow gets addicted to magic in *Buffy the Vampire Slayer*. Dr Faust runs afoul of the devil in folklore and literature. Things even get out of hand for Mickey Mouse in the "Sorcerer's Apprentice" segment of *Fantasia*.

There are also plenty of warnings and cautions in books on practical magic, telling people to be careful, to be clear, to be specific about their needs – because things could go terribly awry if they do the wrong thing, choose the wrong correspondence or make some kind of mistake mid-ritual. And this could be the case. Some folks warn us about threefold or even tenfold returns that could absolutely destroy our lives due to magical backlash.

Most people coming to practical magic are coming from a background that doesn't support magic, usually due to religious strictures, so folks may also have a vague idea that what they are doing is somehow wrong or illicit. At the very least, it may feel like cheating or taking an undeserved shortcut, especially when it comes to money.

These stories and cautions wouldn't exist if they didn't contain a kernel of truth, right? If magic is powerful and can change your life, it could also destroy it, right? Well, yes and no. Stories and concepts like these often perform a specific function. They act as barriers to prevent access to something until the person who knows the story can overcome their fears while simultaneously understanding the real dangers.

For example, imagine being the parent of some unruly children and your family living close to the shores of a dangerous lake. The lake is deep and its water dark. People drown in it every year. You may choose to tell your little children a spooky story about a monster living in the lake. You tell them that a monster that loves to feed on the flesh of children lives in there! Why would you want to do that (besides having a sadistic sense of humour)? If you're lucky, it will keep your little ones far away from the lakeshore. That is, until they get old enough to doubt the story. But once they are old enough to doubt, they are hopefully mature enough to understand the real dangers of the lake and take them seriously. They don't need the made-up danger of a monster any longer. They forget your spooky tale and go on to live productive lives, perhaps resorting to the same story when their children are young.

Except it doesn't always work that way. Images, fears and concepts linger, even when we consciously choose to leave entire belief systems like religions behind. Stories and beliefs are powerful and can continue to affect us on multiple levels of consciousness, even when we don't want them to.

In addition, some people have a specific fear related to working magic for wealth or financial stability. They wonder if working magic for cash will result in a close relative dying and leaving them a hefty inheritance. They fear getting the money they need by directly causing the death of a loved one. That is a heavy concern, and it is one that might drive anyone away from working any kind of money magic, let alone magic for wealth or financial security.

But is it a realistic fear?

The fear of your money magic ending someone's life stems from two different sources.

The first source is a deep-seated belief that it is wrong to want money – the idea that if you do, you are a bad person and are opening yourself up to bad things happening to you. Your selfish desires will result in a deserved comeuppance. I address these kinds of thoughts and beliefs in "Starting from Zero: Identifying and Healing Wealth Wounds" (page 38).

The second source of fear is more subtle, but it is an idea you should consider if you want to be successful in your magical work. Most magicians picture the universe as a bountiful endless source of everything: energy, light and life. A piece of it burns inside each living thing, and we can tap into that source to fuel our magic. It's a beautiful concept but it is something people often forget when they are considering working wealth magic.

If you work a spell for enlightenment, you don't fear that the people around you will suddenly get less enlightened if your spell is a success. If you work a spell for protection, you don't fear that a member of your family will suddenly, inexplicably become unsafe. We consider things like enlightenment and safety boundless and bountiful. But when it comes to money, we tend to lock ourselves into the idea that wealth is, by necessity, limited. That leads to the fear that obtaining enough or even more than enough (what horror) will lead to someone else suffering or losing out.

If we expand the idea of wealth to cover all the resources we need, physical and spiritual, you'll see that the idea of material wealth being somehow limited or tied to someone else's loss doesn't make a lot of sense in the grand scheme of things.

Fears intertwined with practical magic and wealth magic in particular can work against your magical efforts. When you are completing spells and rituals for any purpose, the most important thing you can do is align your mind, heart and soul with your goals. You can't do that if you are afraid of the results.

If you decide to work through "Starting from Zero: Identifying and Healing Wealth Wounds" (page 38), you will have the opportunity to think more deeply about any hidden fears you have related to the magical and mundane pursuit of wealth.

Proving yourself right (in the worst way)

"Tell me a spell to make me win the lottery!" That's a request I've received several times from magic users and non-magic users alike over the years. I've read tarot cards, and "tell me the winning lottery numbers" is something I hear with equal regularity.

When these questions come from non-magic users, I take it as someone having a little bit of fun at my expense, which is fine. I have a sarcastic sense of humour, and though I've heard the joke what seems like a million times, I can give the person a smirk and say, "But that means I won't win this time." Problem solved.

But when questions like these come from magically or spiritually minded people, I fear that they indicate what I call a "So there!" attitude hiding somewhere deep within their souls.

Some folks have a tendency to approach money or wealth magic by picking the grandest spell they can find and setting an intention like "I want to be financially stable and well off by the end of the year." They work the spell; they sit back and wait . . . and nothing happens. Or maybe they get a small amount of money, their hopes rise, but then nothing else occurs.

Then they decide money magic doesn't work for them and totally abandon the idea. Perhaps they choose to believe that money is too base a thing to work magic for. Maybe they suspect that they are flawed in some way or that's just the way it goes.

What I suspect is happening is that some part of their subconscious or some little voice at the back of their mind whispers, "This wealth magic thing can't really work. I'll ask for something over-the-top and it won't work. I will prove it to myself once and for all."

They fling their spell out into the universe with a subconscious "So there!" attached to it. And you know what? They prove themselves right!

Wealth magic won't work for them – but not because it is flawed magic, or they don't deserve it. It won't work because they are secretly working to prove to themselves that it doesn't.

In a world where poverty and plenty grow wider apart by the second, I am the last person to believe that a simple spell or two is going to help anyone become a millionaire overnight. But I do think that understanding yourself, setting goals and using magic to support your intentions goes a long way to improving someone's circumstances.

So watch out for that "So there!" attitude. Approach wealth magic with an open mind.

STARTING FROM ZERO: IDENTIFYING AND HEALING WEALTH WOUNDS

All the concepts listed in this section can be contributing factors that create or exacerbate wealth wounds. The term sounds dramatic, but wealth wounds are simply damaging beliefs about wealth that have been internalized. They can subtly (and sometimes not so subtly) impact your self-image and the ways you conceptualize and deal with prosperity and wealth.

These types of wounds can be the most significant barriers to working successful wealth magic. As a wise magician, you already know that working to identify and heal your personal wealth wounds will go a long way toward improving your finances and assist you with achieving your financial goals.

DEFINING WEALTH WOUNDS

Wealth wounds –
Internalized beliefs about prosperity or wealth that are limiting or negative, and that may obstruct financial success and the performance of effective wealth magic. They can originate from internal and external sources and can arise at any point in life. Varying in severity, they may not appear to be directly connected to financial or prosperity matters at first glance. However, they affect your overall relationship with wealth and abundance.

HOW WE GET WEALTH WOUNDS

There are countless types of wealth wounds, and there are innumerable ways to get them. It isn't an exaggeration to say that each and every wealth wound is specific to the individual. Two people can experience the same thing yet walk away with markedly different impressions of what happened. Some of the experiences I list below might make perfect sense to you. Others may leave you puzzled, wondering what could be so terrible about them. That is because we have each had different experiences in our lives up to this point.

Potential causes of wealth wounds include:

- Growing up with little money or few resources
- Experiencing a financial crisis at some point in your life, either as a child or an adult
- Job loss
- Homelessness
- Knowing someone who is super-wealthy but is also a jerk
- Getting bullied or mistreated by someone you perceive as wealthy or prosperous
- Watching another family or a loved one struggle with financial difficulties
- Being the victim of a theft or scam
- Being the victim of a bad work environment
- Being the victim of any kind of abuse
- Conflicting or negative messages about prosperity or wealth from authority figures in your life
- Dropping out of school
- Debt

It is also important to note that though I have listed individual causes, a combination of events, experiences and beliefs can contribute to a single wealth wound. Or one person may suffer from multiple wounds.

Here is an example from my personal life.

Though I went to university, I ran out of money, patience and mental health and so decided to drop out. I already felt terrible about what I was doing, but to say my parents were unhappy about my decision would be an understatement. As any parent would, they had major concerns about what this meant for my future, particularly about how well I would be able to support myself. They expressed these concerns in ways that were damaging to my self-esteem and my self-confidence. From these expressions, I internalized messages like "Dee's not smart enough to get along in life", "Dee isn't going to find a well-paying job" and "Dee won't ever be financially secure".

Those beliefs combined to cause a major wealth wound that I had to spend a lot of energy and time healing. Of course, there is always a silver lining. The healing process taught me a lot about how to identify the other wealth wounds from which I was suffering and how to go about healing them.

TECHNIQUES TO IDENTIFY AND HEAL WEALTH WOUNDS

For some folks, just reading the term "wealth wound" may call to mind several things. If you are one of those people, good for you, because a small part of your work is done already. Notice I said a *small* part of your work. I say that for two reasons:

1. Identifying wealth wounds is only the first step to fully healing them.
2. If you quickly identify one or two, it may convince you that those are the *only* two you are currently dealing with. That may or may not be the case, so resist the urge to proceed without further reflection.

If you are one of those folks whose intuition didn't immediately serve up a selection of wealth wounds for you to examine, do not fear! For most people, it takes time and reflection to identify their wealth wounds.

A couple of warnings before you start:

- Only you can identify your wealth wounds. That means that you shouldn't take anyone's opinions about your personal issues too seriously, unless they are your therapist or a close loved one who has your best interests at heart. It also means that you shouldn't impose your opinion on someone else if they are attempting to identify their wealth wounds. If you are invited to assist or give your opinions, do so in a gentle and thoughtful way.

- I have found the process of identifying and healing wealth wounds to be continual. Once you heal one issue, another may arise in its place. Also, just because you are working on healing your wealth wounds doesn't mean you won't suffer new ones. So prepare to revisit these techniques.

Below are some simple ways you can begin the identification process.

Journalling

I am sure you have probably heard this before, but it bears repeating. Journalling is a wonderful way to sort out your thoughts and discover important information about yourself. Whether you regularly journal or not, you can spend some time with pen and paper (or keyboard and mouse) to reflect on your relationship with wealth.

If you aren't sure where to start, pick one of the prompts below and write about it for at least five minutes.

- What is my earliest memory about money? How did it make me feel?
- How secure did I feel growing up?
- How do the important people in my life talk about money?
- What causes me the most anxiety about my financial situation?
- What does abundance mean to me?
- What parts of my life am I grateful for?
- What part of my life would I change if I could change only one thing? Why?

The next day, carefully review what you wrote. It may spawn more questions or ideas that you want to explore in future journal entries. Or it could point toward a wealth wound that is causing you difficulties. Further contemplation and journalling can heal the wounds you identify, or you might wish to try one of the other methods in this section.

Talking about it

Talking through your feelings about money and prosperity can be exceptionally helpful while you are attempting to identify your wealth wounds. Sometimes just hearing yourself say something out loud can trigger astonishing insights into your experiences. The process can be both cathartic and eye-opening. Hearing a second perspective on your experiences may also provide useful insights.

You may choose to discuss your thoughts and feelings about prosperity and wealth informally with a friend or family member. Or you could decide to address these topics with a professional counsellor or therapist. Either way, make sure that whomever you are talking to understands your goal and what you want to accomplish. You don't have to tell them this is part of a magical process if you aren't comfortable sharing that information (particularly if you don't think the idea will be well received). But you can tell them about your goals for exploring your feelings about money and wealth, and how you want to better understand yourself to plan for your future.

Energy and body work

We often store stress from trauma and anxieties in our bodies or the energy fields that surround them. Sensing how spiritual energy flows through and around your body allows you to identify energy blockages and issues like wealth wounds.

Intentional movements like yoga, walking meditations or mindfulness exercises help familiarize you with your body. These practices help release blocked energy and stimulate the energy flow through you.

Energy- or aura-healing work can do the same, allowing you to balance and regulate your personal energy flow.

Often, after the energy blockages are cleared, you will receive intuitive knowledge that will provide you with a deeper understanding of issues like wealth wounds, which you can then continue to work to resolve.

Meditation and visualization

Targeted meditation and visualization can be invaluable tools for identifying wealth wounds. Meditation allows you to clear your mind and become open to messages from your intuition and the universe at large. Visualization allows you to take a symbolic journey to seek out the information you need. These two techniques can work together to help you better understand and resolve the deep-seated beliefs that affect your relationship with prosperity and wealth.

MINDFUL STRETCHING
FOR WEALTH WOUNDS

1. Sit, stand or lie down, whichever is the most comfortable to you.
2. Allow yourself to become physically still.
3. Take several deep, slow breaths at a rate that is comfortable to you. Don't strain to hold your breaths for long or to inhale as much air as you physically can. Do this breathing to relax yourself for the work ahead.
4. When you feel relaxed, announce what you are doing. I usually phrase this like I am talking to myself. I say something like, "Today I am going to stretch to adjust and regulate my energy. I seek to release blockages and redirect energy where it needs to be. I am open to receiving messages to help me with my goal of identifying my wealth wounds."
5. Your attention will naturally be drawn to a part of your body that feels sore, stiff or sluggish.
6. Gently stretch that area in a way that feels good to you. You may wish to rotate that joint, extend that limb, or shift your body to relieve the tension or invigorate the area. Work on that area until you feel your work there is complete.
7. Wait to see if your attention is drawn to a different part of your body.
8. Repeat steps 6 and 7 until you feel your session is complete.
9. Take several deep breaths to come back to everyday waking reality.
10. Drink some cool water.

While you are stretching, releasing blockages and readjusting your body's energy flow, you may receive a flood of information about a variety of topics, including wealth wounds. Or your mind may remain blissfully still and focused on what you are doing. More often than not it takes some time for the energetic changes to take full effect. You will intuit information as your body continues to adjust to the alterations in your energy flow.

It is likely that it will take more than one stretching session to identify and heal your wealth wounds. Take your time and allow your body to be your guide.

VISUALIZATION FOR
WEALTH WOUNDS

This technique starts with a meditation session to clear and calm your mind, and then moves on to a visualization session to help you diagnose and heal your wealth wounds. Just like the mindful stretching technique described above, you might receive information during or after your session. You also may need to do this visualization more than once to identify all your wealth wounds.

PREPARATION

1. Choose a time you can work uninterrupted.
2. Dress in comfortable clothing.
3. Create a relaxing atmosphere by burning incense or candles or by playing relaxing music.
4. Have a notebook and pen nearby.

MEDITATION

1. Inhale four times without exhaling. These can be short inhalations, but focus your attention on how your lungs fill up with each intake of air.

2. Slowly exhale all the air in your lungs, releasing all the tension in your body.

3. Repeat steps 1 and 2 at least four times.

4. Breathing slowly and regularly, picture a solid black screen in your mind.

5. In the centre of the screen, picture a small white dot. See it glow in the surrounding darkness.

6. Hold the image of the little dot in the expanse of blackness in your mind for as long as you can. If something distracts you, that's okay. Just bring your attention back to the dot.

7. Watch the dot as it begins to pulse with light, getting brighter when you inhale and dimmer when you exhale. You can stay at this point as long as you like before moving into the visualization proper.

VISUALIZATION

1. When you are ready, see yourself flying closer and closer to the little white dot. As you get closer, it will expand into an opening large enough for you to pass through.

2. As you move through the opening, you see a brightly lit, clean and welcoming room filled with a golden light.

3. In the centre of the room, you see a table. On the table you see a representation of your energetic body. It could look exactly like you. It could look like a glowing cloud of fog. It might look like a mythical creature or a baby. The appearance doesn't matter.

4. Spend some time examining and celebrating what your energy body looks like to you. Know that it probably doesn't look like this every day and that another energy worker may see it completely differently. However, this is the form you will work with today.

5. When you feel ready, begin to scan your energy body for areas of congested energy flow, dark spots or other things that indicate areas of concern. As you do so, be aware of any feelings or messages you may intuit.

SETTING THE SCENE

6.   Take note of each area of concern. If it feels right, work to heal each area by sending warm golden energy to it with the intent of resolving the issue. If you don't feel inclined to try to resolve it, you don't need to at this point and can just observe.

7.   When you are finished with your analysis, return to full consciousness by telling yourself you will awake by counting down from five to one, obtaining full consciousness at one. Perform the countdown.

8.   After you awaken, make sure to note down your experiences and observations for future reference.

HEALING WEALTH WOUNDS

As you can probably already imagine, some wealth wounds are easier to heal than others. The odd thing is that sometimes the oldest wounds, which you might suspect are the strongest and most difficult to resolve, heal quickly and easily. That's because by the time you examine some of those older beliefs, your current perspective has developed to the point that the wealth wound and the issue embedded in it seem completely ridiculous. If that is the case, sometimes just identifying the wound and examining it heals it completely.

Here is an example from a friend of mine.

A friend I'll call Jack had a bad relationship early in life. You know the kind. Their partner was selfish, and their needs always had to come first. My friend's needs were ignored and minimized. My friend was called on to cater to their partner and make sure they always had what they needed.

From this relationship, Jack internalized the message that they weren't important. They suffered a wealth wound that told them their needs were never significant enough to pay attention to.

Jack carried that wound for a long time. I am happy to say that Jack went on to have relationships that were much healthier and more supportive. As he continued to mature, he had a much better understanding of the importance of his needs.

By the time Jack got around to examining the wealth wounds he was still carrying with him and discovered a wound saying that his needs weren't important and didn't need to be met, it only took a small amount of work to heal that wound. He recognized it as an outdated belief that was never correct in the first place.

Conversely, quite a bit of time and effort often goes into healing more recent wealth wounds. If you have received the wound recently, it may be more difficult to treat yourself with the compassion and understanding you need to heal.

SETTING THE SCENE

For example, if I just lost my long-term, well-loved job last week, causing me great anxiety and fear about my future, it will take more energy and effort to work through and resolve the issues embedded in the wound.

It takes time

Though you are likely eager to heal all your wealth wounds and move past them, it will take time to identify all of them and to work through healing each one. As I mentioned above, some wounds will heal quickly and easily, while others may take quite a bit of effort to work through. Each one is a learning process that will allow you to better understand yourself, so it is important that you give each wealth wound the time and attention it needs to fully heal.

It takes repetition

Some wealth wounds resolve after an initial effort. Others are persistent. It is hard to predict which ones will disappear after that first try and which will hang around like unwanted guests at the end of a party. As much as you can, don't fall into the trap of expectations. Acknowledge each wealth wound and decide to work on it until it is healed, no matter how long it takes. Your journey to healing is your journey and no one else's. It may not be linear. It certainly isn't a race against anyone else or against your previous accomplishments. Take whatever time is needed to heal.

Prioritization

Most folks have more than one wealth wound. If you find yourself with a list of issues to confront, don't despair! My advice for choosing which issue to work on first is simple. Pick whatever issue interests you the most. You'll likely feel drawn to one. If that's the case, work on it. Or you might be interested in working on an issue because it seems so surprising to you that it exists. If so, work on that one!

As you confront, explore and heal one wealth wound, you might just find

THE GOLDEN GRIMOIRE

that other wounds resolve themselves. So the only way to begin untangling the ball of thread is to find an end and start gently tugging on it. Your intuition will guide you.

WORKING WEALTH MAGIC WHEN YOU HAVE WEALTH WOUNDS

After all this discussion about wealth wounds, you might be wondering if it is even possible to work money, prosperity and wealth magic when you have them. It certainly is! If not, no one would ever be able to work wealth magic, because we are all receiving and dealing with wealth wounds throughout our lives. It is an ongoing process.

However, the more attention you give to healing your wealth wounds, particularly those you picked up at an early age, the easier wealth magic becomes. You do not have to resolve "all" your wealth wounds before working wealth magic. But it is important to dedicate some effort to resolving them while you are doing so.

WEALTH WOUND CLEANSING BATH/ SHOWER AND BLESSING

While meditation, reflection and journalling can help heal and mitigate your wealth wounds, there's nothing like adding a little magic to your healing process to support your efforts. This magical cleansing technique is paired with a blessing that fills up the void left by banishing disruptive influences.

This blessing works best after you have worked through the material about wealth wounds on page 38.

LOCATION
Your bathroom, of course! You can perform this cleansing ritual while showering or bathing, whichever you prefer. I think it works best when you can soak in a tub.

TIMING
It's my philosophy that our busy lives require us to fit healing and self-care in whenever we can. However, if you have the chance, take this bath on a Wednesday or Sunday when the moon is waning.

Note:

Cleaning your bathroom is often recommended before doing any kind of ritual bathing. This is so that you create a pure, clear and relaxing space in which to bathe. I agree with this idea wholeheartedly, but if you don't have the time or energy, don't let this suggestion stop you from ritual bathing. Sometimes, if you wait for the perfect conditions, you never get started. So clean if you are able, but proceed without cleaning if you must.

SUPPLIES

- Salt
- Two cups of Epsom salts (two heaped tablespoons if showering)
- Rosemary essential oil – clarify your mind
- Lemongrass essential oil – purification
- Cedarwood essential oil – grounding
- Bergamot essential oil – uplifting
- Candle or candles in your favourite colour
- A small bowl
- A washcloth (if showering)
- A hair tie or rubber band (if showering)

STEPS FOR A BATH

1. Prepare your bathroom. If possible, get rid of clutter and give the surfaces a scrub.
2. As this is a ritual bath, it is helpful to take a shower beforehand. That way you don't have to worry about grooming and can focus on the spiritual aspects of the bath. So, if you choose, take a short shower first.
3. Put your candles in a safe place and light them. If you want to bathe by candlelight, feel free. But wait to turn off your electric lights until you are done with step 5.
4. Turn on some relaxing music.
5. Before running the water for the bath, make your cleansing mixture:
   - Put three large pinches of salt in the bowl.
   - Put two cups of Epsom salts in the bowl. Say, "Creatures of earth, heal my wounds and cleanse my soul."
   - Put 2–5 drops of rosemary essential oil in the bowl. Say, "Friend of memory, clarify my mind."
   - Put 2–5 drops of lemongrass essential oil in the bowl. Say, "Friend of purity, cleanse my aura."
   - Put 2–5 drops of cedarwood essential oil in the bowl. Say, "Friend of healing, dispel my pains."
   - Stir the mixture with your hands while picturing what you

want the bath to do for you (remove anxiety, heal existing wealth wounds, change your attitude about money, etc.)

6. Run your bathwater. It should be pleasantly warm but not scalding hot.

7. While the water fills the tub, cast handfuls of the salt mixture into the water, saying, "Cleanse me and heal me, dispel all disruptive influences."

8. When the tub is full and the salt mixture is completely dissolved, climb into the bath and submerge as much of yourself as possible.

9. Once you get settled in the tub, take some deep, calming breaths. Allow your muscles to relax.

10. Now comes the real work. Close your eyes and identify the areas of pain and discomfort in your body. These may be physical pains or problem areas located in the aura that surrounds your body. Or they could be emotional concerns that trouble your heart or mind. Pay attention to how each one feels. Do you feel a literal soreness? Does it feel like an electric tingle? Maybe it feels like a heavy weight. Identify each issue and how it feels.

11. Select one of the pain points. Focus on it and picture it. Then visualize the power of the bath resolving and healing the issue. (I often see it as a dark, complex knot being untied and dissolved, but it's different for everyone!)

12. One by one, address each pain point and picture the bath working its magic and banishing all disruptive, painful or otherwise upsetting influences.

13. Remain in the bath for at least 20 minutes.

14. If you don't mind getting your hair wet, submerge your head at least three times.

15. When you are ready, stand up and climb out of the tub. As you allow the water to drain, picture all your difficulties and pains going down the drain with the water and flowing far, far away from you.

16. If necessary, wrap your hair up in a towel, but allow the rest of your body to air dry. (You can throw on a robe, just don't towel off.)

THE GOLDEN GRIMOIRE

STEPS FOR A SHOWER

Follow the steps above, but instead of making a bowl of cleansing salts, use a washcloth and a hair tie or rubber band to create a scrubbing bundle.

1. Spread the washcloth out on a firm surface.
2. Make the salt mixture in the centre of the washcloth.
   Use about 2–3 tablespoons of Epsom salts.
3. Gather the corners of the washcloth and use the
   hair tie or rubber band to secure it.
4. Turn on the water and adjust the temperature.
5. After identifying your pain points, begin to
   scrub yourself with the salt bundle.
6. Start at the top of your head and work your way down to your
   feet. As you encounter areas of your body that have pain points,
   visualize the power of the salt bundle dissolving the issues.
   See them melt off you and wash away down the drain.

Follow up with a blessing

Whether you took a bath or a shower, you have now banished powers, ideas and beliefs that no longer serve you. Use this blessing to fill up the space that is left. You can do this blessing in the bathroom, or you can wait until you dry off and do it at an altar or other workspace. Use one of the candles that you burned during your cleansing bath.

1. Place a candle in your favourite colour in front of you.
2. Carefully warm your hands near the glow of the candle's flames. Picture the power and strength of the flame entering your body and filling you with a pure white fire.
3. Pour a small amount of bergamot essential oil that has been diluted into a carrier oil into your palm or a small glass. If you don't wish to use an essential oil, you can use blessed water.
4. Spend a moment breathing in the uplifting scent of the oil.
5. Close your eyes and see the oil in your hands shining with a soft golden glow.
6. If you wish to work with a deity or other entity, say a short prayer or invite them to bless the oil.
7. Using the bergamot oil or blessed water, anoint your forehead, throat, heart, back of your neck, wrists, and tops and bottoms of your feet. As you do, say, "I welcome in blessings and positive powers to shower me with prosperity and wealth."

TAKING INVENTORY AND COUNTING BLESSINGS

In this section, you will find a few techniques to help prepare you for your journey to a wealthier and more prosperous life. Dedicating time to understanding your current financial situation can help prepare you to make important decisions about your budget and financial plans.

KNOW WHERE YOU ARE TO GET WHERE YOU WANT TO GO

When starting out on any journey, before you decide where you want to go and how you want to get there, you need to know where you are. Even when you already have a general idea of where you stand, this can be a daunting proposition when it comes to your finances. There is so much to take into consideration, particularly if you feel as though you are in a stable situation but want to make improvements. However, it is worth taking the time to figure it out. Understanding your starting point will give you a baseline against which you can compare your results. It can also open your eyes to things that you want to change or improve upon.

SETTING THE SCENE

ACKNOWLEDGING WHAT IS ON YOUR SIDE

Starting on a positive note is important. As you begin to assess your current financial state, try to avoid immediately focusing on all your problems or all the things you think are going wrong. If you are like me, you worry about your problems enough already. To give yourself a boost, begin by concentrating on all the positive things that are working in your favour *right now*. Not the stuff you hope to accomplish. Not the things that might happen soon. Pay attention to all the good things that are a part of your life now, particularly as they relate to your prosperity.

Gratitude and generosity are two important features of successful wealth magic. Regularly reviewing your present situation and acknowledging the things you can be grateful for helps to establish a positive mindset and cultivate a perspective that will allow you to be generous to others.

Speaking as a natural pessimist, I understand if you are rolling your eyes right now. I really do. I was born a glass-half-empty person. It contributes to a wealth wound that I am still hard at work healing. I know that some people reading these words may be in dire financial situations that seem bleak and hopeless. But I know from going through a few situations like that myself, there is always at least one thing that is on your side, even if it is only your sheer determination to claw your way out of your difficulties.

Also, I have discovered that once you are able to identify one positive thing, it becomes easier to identify others. So that means it is time to start a list. If you have a diary or magical journal, that's the perfect place to start a fresh page of notes on all the positive things that are supporting your financial goals right now. If you don't have a book to write in, no biggie! Grab a spare piece of paper and get started.

Give the page a heading that appeals to you, like "Gratitude List" or "The Good Stuff" or whatever you like. Over the course of a week, spend five or ten minutes per day thinking about and noting down what is helping to sustain you. The things you list *do not* need to be material items like money in the bank or a car. They can be anything that you are grateful for.

Your list may look something like this:

1. A roof over my head
2. Some money in savings
3. My job/paycheque (even if you aren't grateful for your job all the time, you can always be grateful for the money it generates!)
4. My best friend
5. My roommate
6. The view out my window
7. My phone
8. My health

Throughout the week, ideas may come to you when you aren't near your notebook. Be sure to scribble them down somewhere and copy them onto your list when you can.

At the end of the week, read through the list. Think about each item on it and realize the value it brings to your life. Send a message of gratitude to the universe for all that you have.

UNDERSTANDING WHAT IS WORKING AGAINST YOU

Once you have acknowledged all the things that are on your side and helping you attain your financial goals, it is time to take a realistic look at the not-so-good side of things. The difficult part of this exercise is making sure you keep things realistic and don't fall prey to catastrophic thinking. Yes, a scary disaster could loom up out of nowhere and totally derail things tomorrow. But this exercis e isn't about that kind of attitude. Instead, it's about taking an honest accounting of what you are working against or need to resolve. It might even include things you want but don't yet have.

Just like when you took account of what was working for you, this is going to be a real list that you write down so you can go back and look at it later. (If you are the kind of person that finds crossing things off lists satisfying, you will be thrilled when you get to do so with this list!) You can make this list in your diary or magical journal or on a spare piece of paper. Give it a heading like "Challenges" or "Things to Overcome". Remember that you can include items on the list that may not be related to material or financial concerns.

Your list may look something like this:

1. Student loan debt
2. Unreliable work schedule
3. Credit card debt
4. No car
5. High rent
6. Anxiety over filing taxes

Spend a week adding to the list. The results may surprise you. I often find that once I put things down in a list, they don't seem as big and overwhelming.

Every single thing you put on this list is a candidate for setting a financial goal that magic can help you accomplish. You can prioritize the list and decide the order in which you want to resolve these issues. If you aren't sure where to start, meditate on it for a while, or talk to a trusted friend or family member who has their financial situation in order and ask for some advice.

THE GOLDEN GRIMOIRE

FINANCIAL ADVICE AND ADVISORS

At any point in your efforts to improve your finances, if you feel so confused you are unable to proceed on your own, please don't hesitate to reach out for help. There are plenty of resources available, including information online, advice from friends and family, and assistance from professionals. If you are looking for a professional to help you, a good place to start is your bank. There are experts there who are available to discuss how to meet your financial needs. Your bank may also be able to point you to other free resources in your community. A quick search online can also be helpful. A little bit of research can help you find numerous allies. If you need help picking the right person for you, consider trying the Dowsing To Find the Right Help method on page 265.

SETTING YOUR INTENTIONS: MINDFUL BUDGETING AND FINANCIAL PLANNING

The most important thing to understand about budgeting and financial planning is that they are two different things with two very different goals.

Budget –
A detailed plan for allocating your income to regularly occurring expenses, paying off your debts and contributing to your savings. The goal of a budget is to manage your daily expenses. Most personal budgets are calculated monthly, but some folks choose to use a weekly or biweekly basis, depending on how they are paid.

Financial plan –
A comprehensive plan that includes your budget but also includes things like long-term savings and investing goals, wealth management and retirement planning. Financial plans span decades rather than days or weeks.

When you create a budget or financial plan for yourself, you need to take into consideration your definition of wealth, your values and your needs.

Planning your financial future is a deeply personal process that should take your spiritual beliefs and personal attitudes into account. Formulate your goals using a holistic approach that considers your quality of life, your wellbeing and the needs of your loved ones.

When you are in the planning stages, you have the chance to explore your desires, your hopes and what motivates you. Don't allow yourself to be swayed by the opinions of others. Their ideas of wealth may not match your understanding of it.

FIGURING OUT WHAT YOU WANT AND HOW TO GET THERE

Take the time to ask yourself questions about how you want to live your life going forward. Is it important for you to amass wealth to pass on to future generations? Or are you more interested in earning enough to travel the world? Do you want a career that brings you fame as well as fortune? Or do you just want to be left alone to live your life?

Allowing yourself time to think and dream about your future will prevent you from experiencing a series of false starts and frustrations. There is nothing worse than rushing part way to one goal and then suddenly changing direction when you realize that isn't what you really want out of life. Patiently thinking through your options will give you the confidence to pursue your goals in the face of obstacles and disappointments.

GOAL-SETTING

Once you know what you want, you will increase your chances of getting it by setting goals. Though you might be tempted to leave your goals as vague statements like "I'll have enough money to move soon", consider using the SMART approach to goal-setting.

This method was created by George T Doran in the early 1980s and is heavily used in the business world. But it can be easily adapted to your personal life.

The SMART goal method says your goals should be:

- **Specific** – Your goal should be clearly stated and easily understood. If you aren't sure how to word your goal, ask yourself who, what, where, when, why and how. For example, my goal might be to save $500 to use as spending money during my vacation next August.
- **Measurable** – Your goal should be measurable. Usually, if you make

the goal specific enough, it will be measurable. In my example above, I can monitor my savings account, my piggy bank or the strongbox under my bed and know exactly how much of the $500 I have already saved.

◦ **Achievable** – There is no point in setting a goal that can't be obtained in a reasonable amount of time. Why? Because there is a chance you'll get frustrated and give up before you reach it! If you have a big goal, break it down into smaller, more achievable goals so that you can track your progress more easily and build on your successes. If I am completely strapped for cash and can only save $10 per month, I might have to reevaluate my goal and adjust it so I don't set a hopeless task for myself.

◦ **Relevant** – It might seem silly to have to say it, but your goal should be relevant to your desires and your plans for the future. Your goal should align with your overall objectives, and its accomplishment should bring you one step closer to what you want to achieve. It should be something that is important to you and that you feel driven to accomplish. If I wasn't going on vacation in August, or if I really wanted to buy an expensive new book instead, then my goal isn't relevant to my current desires, and I run the risk of abandoning it.

◦ **Time-bound** – Your goal should have a deadline so that you have some motivation for getting it done. My example goal has a built-in deadline – August. This lets me know how much I need to accomplish each day, week and month to achieve the goal in time. Setting deadlines helps build a sense of commitment and greatly increases the chance of you achieving goals.

Please note that I use this method for creating my goals but not for creating my magical intentions. I prefer to give the universe room to work when I set my magical intentions, so I try not to be too specific about how my desires will come to pass. However, I can use my SMART goal to help me understand what I can visualize in magical workings to support my goal. In the example I used above, I would picture myself on vacation with that $500 (or more) in my wallet and ready to spend!

MAGICAL BUDGETING RITUAL AND WORKSHEET

This ritual is all about taking control of your budget and finances. If you use it for budgeting, it will give you a deeper understanding of where your money is going each month and how much you are spending on necessary and not-so-necessary items.

Though creating a personal budget can be stressful, the point of this ritual is to make budgeting and planning sacred acts that honour your hard work and acknowledge your current situation. You can use this ritual as a first step to making friends with your finances and getting comfortable with thinking about them objectively.

Some things to consider before you start:

- A good budget is flexible. If possible, try to avoid allocating every single part of your income. Leave a portion free to help cover unexpected expenses.
- If you don't know how much you spend in a particular category, it's okay to estimate. As you track your spending from month to month, you can update information as necessary.
- There are two different ways to approach drafting a budget. Neither is better than the other, but one may appeal to you more.

  1. You can simply note down on average what you are spending in each category and then make choices about what you would like to change. For example, you may realize that you spend too much on dining out or impulse buying. Over time, you can make changes to your spending habits and update your budget to reflect those changes.
  2. You can start by writing down what you expect to spend in each category and then attempt to adhere to those guidelines from the start. Depending on the complexity of your budget, this may be an easier approach.

SETTING THE SCENE

TIMING
A quiet, peaceful time on a Wednesday.

SUPPLIES
- A canldle in your favourite colour
- A white candle
- Scrap paper
- Olive oil or Abundant Wealth Oil (page 247)
- A pencil
- Personal prosperity sigil (page 110) (optional)
- A cup of your favourite beverage
- Comfortable clothing
- Financial information like your income, expenses and debts
- Magical Budgeting Worksheet

STEPS

1. Choose a working space that gives you plenty of room to spread out. I usually use my dining room table because my office desk is too cluttered to hold everything comfortably.
2. Arrange your supplies in a way that is aesthetically pleasing to you. Make sure you position the candles in a place where you won't knock them over.
3. Go put on some comfy clothing that you love.
4. Pour yourself your favourite drink to enjoy while you work.
5. Put on some relaxing music.
6. Light the candle that represents you. Say something like, "Calm and clear, relaxed and composed, I build my future as I go."
7. Light the white candle. Say something like, "Blessed light, be my guide and show me the way to a balanced budget."
8. State your intent. It can be something like, "Tonight I will draft a monthly budget." Or, "Today I will create a budget to help me save $100 a month."
9. Anoint each of the four corners of your scrap paper

with a tiny dab of olive oil or Abundant Wealth Oil.
Say, "Focus my thoughts and guide my efforts."

10. If you choose to use your personal prosperity sigil, draw it at the top of the paper. Place the hand you write with palm down on top of the sigil. Envision the energy of the sigil infusing the paper.

11. Using the Magical Budgeting Worksheet as a reference, start gathering information on your scrap paper.

12. Once you have the information you need, anoint the four corners of the worksheet with the olive oil or Abundant Wealth Oil (if you are going to record the information on a digital spreadsheet, dip your finger in the oil and just point to the four corners of your computer screen). Say something like, "This budget I build to accomplish these financial goals: [state goals]."

13. Fill in the information on your Magical Budgeting Worksheet.

14. If you choose to work with a spiritual ally, pray or speak to them to ask for their help adhering to your budget or plan.

15. Leave your completed worksheet in front of the candles (at a safe distance) and let them burn as long as possible. (If you completed your worksheet on your computer, you can skip this step or let your candle burn near your machine.)

The most important part of creating a budget, magical or otherwise, is to revisit it often to see how well you are sticking to it. At least once a month, update your budget with your current spending and see how it compares to your expectations.

SETTING THE SCENE

FOUNDATIONS OF
FINANCIAL MAGIC

TAROT: A HELPFUL TOOL DURING YOUR FINANCIAL JOURNEY

When it comes to dealing with finances, the future is often unclear. Are we heading in the right direction, running around in circles or about to hit a brick wall? It can seem as though every decision is crucial and any wrong step could lead to disaster. Luckily, that perception is often based more on anxiety than reality.

To help settle your nerves, you can grab a trusty pack of tarot cards to discover the roots of your current situation and chart a route to a future of prosperous wealth. As each tarot image can evoke many different meanings, this chapter includes helpful card layouts as well as interpretations specific to readings about money and finances. You can use these focused interpretations in conjunction with standard card meanings with the layouts in this chapter or in readings you create on your own.

TAKE A HEALTHY APPROACH

Before we get started, this is a good place to reflect on the purpose of Tarot and how to use it in a healthy way. Whether you are reading cards for yourself or having someone read cards for you, please remember that the locus of control should remain with you and not with the cards or the reader. Tarot is an excellent tool for giving you advice and helping you to gain a different perspective on a situation, but it shouldn't be making decisions for you. Someone reading cards for you should not be telling you what to do. They should be providing you with information which you will then use to make decisions. Don't give up your power by letting a tool or a person take away your ability to choose. Absorb what the cards have to say, compare it with your perceptions and determine your best course of action.

The use of Tarot doesn't replace good advice from an expert, whether that person is a professional or simply a friend who has been in a similar situation. So, while divination can be an informative part of your financial-planning process, it shouldn't be your only tool. Read the cards, but also commit yourself to doing real-world research, consulting with experts and discussing your plans with other people you trust.

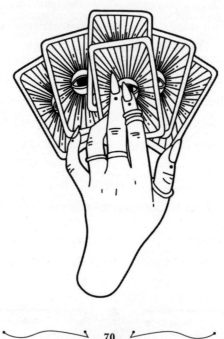

DIY DIVINATION

You may have been told that it's nearly impossible to do your own divination, especially when it comes to topics that are extremely important to you or emotionally charged. Please believe that this is not the case. It may not be quite as easy, but you can do it if you keep these tips in mind.

1. Plan your questions carefully. Even if you are using one of the spreads below, it is important for you to focus your intent on what it is you want to know. However, it's also a good idea to keep the question open-ended so you will receive as much information as possible. For example, ask, "What do I need to know about getting that job I want?" rather than "Will I get that job?" The first version of the question leaves you open to finding out that even if you do get the job, you may not like it, or that there is another, better opportunity lurking around the corner.

2. Write your question down and write down the answer as it develops. Writing down the question forces you to make it concrete. Taking notes about the answer as it grows throughout the reading helps you to remain objective.

3. As you interpret the cards, ask yourself how you would verbalize the answer to a good friend if they asked the questions. Don't let the answer remain as vague ideas in your mind.

4. Learn to be thankful for all the information you receive, whether it is what you wanted to hear or not. If it's confirmation things are going to be fine, be grateful for that. If it's a dire warning about future events, be grateful you know in advance and can take steps to avoid or reduce the impact.

5. Don't forget that you are a magician! You can change your fate with some pre-planning and some well-thought-out magic. The future is not set in stone, and you have the tools to shape it according to your wishes. So don't ever give up hope.

Finally, as you experiment with the readings in this chapter, you may find what appears to be a positive card in a negative spot or a negative card in a positive spot. For example, you may find that the 2 of Wands reversed lands in a place that is supposed to tell you how to fuel your success. How can "Hesitation. Being unwilling to commit to a direction. Stuck between two options, etc." fuel your success?

You can answer that question in a variety of ways. Here are two of my favourites.

First, you can ask yourself some questions about past experiences and how your hesitation or unwillingness to commit to something has caused difficulties for you. Or you may recall times when being unwilling to commit has saved you from making a mistake. Then you can use those memories to contribute to your understanding.

Second, you can look at the opposite meaning of the 2 of Wands ("Asserting control over your finances. Strategic planning. Reviewing your options. Making important decisions, etc.") and see what light that sheds on your reading.

SEEING SOMETHING YOU DON'T WANT TO SEE

In tackling this issue, refer to item number 5 above. If you see something in your reading that you don't like, remember that the future is not fixed. If it were, why would we use divination? Also, why would we bother with magic? Because if the future was unchanging, magic wouldn't do anything for us. As time, events and influences change, so do our futures. A magician understands where they are, the forces that are in play around and within them, and how to nudge those into new configurations to get what they want. You can use the foreknowledge divination provides to help plan your magical efforts.

Also, no system of divination is perfect. To make your predictions as accurate as possible, combine them with knowledge gathered from other sources. Reflect on them and give yourself time to explore all levels of their symbolism.

LAYOUTS

This section contains just a few of the many layouts you can use to discover what the future holds for your financial plans. Use them as a starting point for exploring your current situation, making plans for the future, and discovering the hidden patterns that will help you make informed decisions.

Preparation

Before performing any of the following readings, follow these steps.

1. Shuffle the cards as you normally do.
2. Concentrate on receiving information about your financial situation.
3. When the time feels right, fan the cards out in front of you, face down.
4. Use your favourite method to select your card(s).
   - Examples: Pulling from the centre of the deck, dealing cards from the top or bottom of the deck, fanning the cards out face down and selecting the cards.

General Outlook (1 card)

Never overlook the simplicity and the focused direction of a one-card pull to see if you are on the right track. Be sure to focus on what you really want to know. Remember that a one-card reading can only tell you so much, so crafting your question is important. It's often a good idea to word your question along the lines of "What do I need to know about [topic]?" or "Give me insight into [topic]."

FOUNDATIONS OF FINANCIAL MAGIC

Financial Forecast (3 cards)

This simple layout can help you identify upcoming events and how they may affect you and your financial stability in the long and short term.

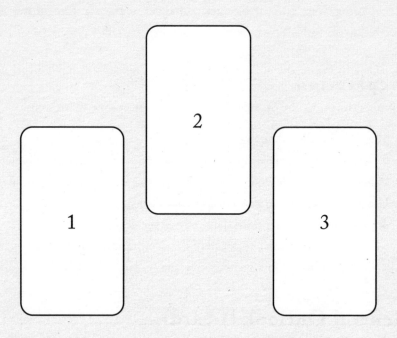

Card 1: Significant Event – What will impact
my finances within the next 1–3 months?

Card 2: Short-Term Impact – How will the event
influence my situation in the short term?

Card 3: Long-Term Impact – How will the event
influence my situation in the long term?

Grow Your Wealth (5 cards)

This layout can help you figure out what is working for and against you as you attempt to improve your financial situation.

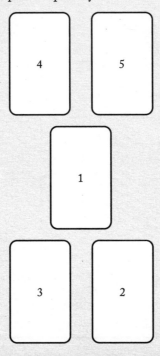

Card 1: **The Seed** – What seed do I need to plant to build my wealth?

Card 2: **The Root** – What preparations do I need to make so that the seed can grow?

Card 3: **The Weed** – What weed(s) do I need to uproot to improve my chances?

Card 4: **The Water** – How will I need to nourish my seed so that it blossoms into wealth?

Card 5: **The Sun** – What will fuel my success?

Turning Fortuna's Wheel (8 cards)

This layout helps you examine a situation and gain a deeper understanding of what you can do to ensure it comes out in your favour.

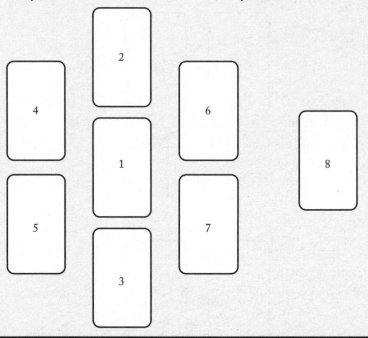

Card 1: – What is the current situation?

Cards 2 and 3: Undecided Influences – What issues, events or people are not currently having an impact on the situation?

Cards 4 and 5: Negative Influences – What issues, events or people are having a negative impact on the situation?

Cards 6 and 7: Positive Influences – What issues, events or people are having a positive impact on the situation?

Card 8: The Handle – How do I get a grasp on the situation, so it turns out how I want it to?

TRUMP/MAJOR ARCANA CARDS: FOCUSED MEANINGS

Trump/Major Arcana cards represent major forces and significant events. With their complex symbolism and striking imagery, each one of the cards in this suit can provide a lot of information. When many trumps appear in a single reading, it indicates an active or chaotic time in which several strong forces are holding sway at once. They might be working together, or they may be at odds. Careful review of the entire layout will help you figure out which of these is the case.

The Fool

Upright – The establishment of a new financial endeavour or business. Making a fresh start, trying something new, and taking necessary but calculated risks to accomplish your goals. Being fearless in the face of uncertainty. Listening to your instincts to make the right choices. Walking your own path instead of following in the footsteps of someone else.

Reversed – Following blind faith rather than thinking things through. Making impulsive financial decisions or being so paralysed with fear that you are unable to make a choice. Not fully understanding the details of a situation or the consequences of your actions. An offer that is too good to be true.

The Magician

Upright – Skilful handling of a business or money matter. Manifestation of your desires through focused efforts. Building bridges between the present and the future. Acting with confidence and flair. A willingness to dazzle people with your expertise and experience. Clear and simple communication provides you with the information you need.

Reversed – Things not being what they seem. Being presented with illusions or false information. An attempt at trickery or deception. A need to view things sceptically. A lack of necessary information. Using caution when making decisions or agreements. Someone who doesn't have your best interests at heart.

The High Priestess

Upright – Listening closely to your intuition and letting it be your guide. Closely guarding your plans. Trusting only a few. Looking beyond the surface of a situation to see things for how they really are. Plumbing your depths to make sure your actions are in accord with your inner wisdom.

Reversed – Consulting with others to make sure you are headed in the right direction. Making sure the facts agree with your intuition. Finding someone you can trust and confide in. Being swayed by strong emotions. Allowing yourself the time to process your feelings before you act.

The Empress

Upright – The availability of abundant resources which will support your efforts. Taking advantage of what is there to make the most of the situation. Ensuring nothing goes to waste. Carefully tending to your financial plans no matter what stage they are in. Maintaining careful attention and nurturing your plans to fruition.

Reversed – Checking your resources to make sure they really are available to you. Confirming that what you need will be there for you when you need it. Conserving your time and energy so you have enough to accomplish your goals. Inability to see the full potential of what is available to you.

The Emperor

Upright – Stepping into your authority and taking control of your finances. Strategy and careful planning can get you where you want to go. Not leaving anything to chance. Being detail-oriented. Being responsible for your current situation and taking the initiative to plan for your future. Maturing into the role of steward of your fortune.

Reversed – Not having control of your finances. Shirking your responsibilities or giving your power to someone else. Feeling disempowered. Avoiding making decisions. Hiding from your responsibilities. Impulsive spending or other risky financial behaviours. Disorganization. Lacking a system for handling your money.

The Hierophant

Upright – Using a well-tested method to handle your finances. Traditional investments or business ventures. Seeking a teacher, mentor or advisor to help you make decisions about your money. Joining an established organization to help you reach your financial goals. Avoiding unconventional or innovative methods. Gathering information in a structured way.

Reversed – The use of unconventional money-management or money-making tools. Breaking free from organizations or stepping away from a mentor or guide to experiment on your own. Embracing innovation and seeking out new developments. Questioning the advice you receive from others. Choosing autonomy over assistance.

The Lovers

Upright – Choosing to either go into partnership with someone or to dissolve a partnership. Considering all your options before deciding. Reaching a crossroad in your financial journey, requiring you to make a choice. Ensuring your business and financial decisions are in harmony with the other parts of your life. Seeking out a collaborator who shares your vision.

Reversed – Conflicts or disagreements with partners or collaborators. An inability or unwillingness to compromise. Questioning the benefits of an existing business or financial relationship. A difference in vision or values. A reassessment of how you are accomplishing your goals. A loss of faith in a partner.

The Chariot

Upright – Increased willpower and determination. Having a clear goal in mind. Feeling driven. The ability to postpone your desires to reach a larger goal. Harnessing your inner strengths to remain true to your goals. Progress. Approaching victory. Encountering and overcoming obstacles.

Reversed – Getting off course. Being sidetracked. Losing control of your financial journey or sight of your goals. Discouragement resulting from trying to do too much too quickly and not seeing the desired results. Obstacles that are difficult to surmount. Sinking time and effort into the wrong aspect of your plan. Travelling in the wrong direction.

Strength

Upright – Resilience and courage to pursue your dreams and do what needs to be done. An ability to wrestle financial obstacles into submission. Finding a way to make your weaknesses work for you rather than against you. Making full use of your talents and strengths. Being your own cheering section. Not needing encouragement from others to get the job done.

Reversed – Struggling to deal with obstacles. Lacking the confidence to approach an issue head-on. Allowing others to control your fortunes. Being overwhelmed by small desires which distract you from achieving your goals. Falling prey to self-doubt. Lacking the determination to put in the necessary time to accomplish your goals.

The Hermit

Upright – Taking time away from everyday routine to introspect. Assessing your progress on your financial journey. Taking a deep dive into a topic. Relying on your own experiences and allowing your inner voice to guide you. Eliminating distractions so you can focus on what is most important.

Reversed – Sticking with the crowd. Being unwilling or unable to allow yourself to blaze your own trail. Following the advice of others. Not trusting your own perceptions. Following a leader or established programme. Avoiding risk. Lack of confidence in your ability to see things how they really are.

The Wheel of Fortune

Upright – An unexpected change for the better. Positive financial outlook. An improvement in cash flow. New opportunities for growth and development of new business plans. A need for adaptability. Being flexible. Adjusting your plans and goals as needed. Staying aware of changing conditions so you can take advantage of them.

Reversed – An unexpected change for the worse. Negative financial outlook. A depletion in cash flow or savings. Difficulty initiating new plans or business ventures. A difficult market that is hard to predict. Inability to adapt to changes. Unreliable contacts. A need for contingency plans.

Justice

Upright – Careful consideration of all the details is required. Taking a holistic approach to your financial plans to ensure all facets are working in harmony. Confidence in your ability to make complex decisions. The search for an equitable outcome for everyone involved. A realistic and detailed analysis of the facts. A search for the truth. Resolution of a court case in your favour.

Reversed – Delayed decision. An inability to ascertain all the facts. Struggling to discover the truth. Feeling out of balance and a lack of harmony with your financial plans. The need for a mediator or adjudicator to help you decide. Resorting to a higher authority. Unwillingness to make a choice. Resolution of a court case but not in your favour.

The Hanged Man

Upright – Putting on the brakes. Suspending immediate actions to assess the situation and gain clarity. Taking the time to think strategically and make solid plans. Looking before you leap. Double-checking the facts before proceeding. Taking time out to help others in need. Gaining an important insight into your finances.

Reversed – Breaking out of a rut. Making your move or putting your plans into action. Getting back to making progress toward your goals. Elimination of delays. Rapid progression. The end of a waiting period. Acting decisively and with confidence. Coming to an end of a period of contemplation or planning.

Death

Upright – Profound transformation of your financial plans. Letting go of outdated ideas or approaches. Making space for new growth. A shift in your perception or plans. The need for adaptability. Releasing old expectations and embracing new dreams. Realigning your plans with your new way of being. Welcoming innovation and renewal.

Reversed – Clinging to the past. Avoiding change. Striving to maintain the status quo. Unwillingness to break old habits and create new ones. A desire for the familiar and the known. Ignoring opportunities for growth. Unwillingness to take risks. Inability to open up to the forces of transformation.

Temperance

Upright – A willingness to experiment. Blending things in new and exciting ways. Striking a balance between opposing forces. Creating harmony where there was none. Coordinating your efforts with others. Prioritization and order. Careful maintenance of balance and proportions. Careful time management. Building a living system that supports your financial objectives.

Reversed – A lack of balance. Being unable to see the whole picture. An inability to make all the pieces of your financial plan work together. A failure of one or more aspects of your plan. Being overburdened or trying to maintain too many things at one time. Lack of prioritization. Loss of proportion. Going to extremes.

The Devil

Upright – Taking an unconventional approach to your finances. Disregarding others' opinions. Wielding power as you see fit. A willingness to turn things upside down to achieve your goals. Running the risk of getting tangled up in your own schemes. A potentially destructive outcome. Debt that is difficult to escape from.

Reversed – Staying on the straight and narrow path. Adhering to the rules and playing by the book. Curbing your desires to reach your goals. Putting yourself in the control of another to achieve your goals. Working to make others comfortable. Taking a conservative approach. Accepting the need for compromise.

The Tower

Upright – Being subjected to upheavals and sudden change. A sudden shock. An event that shakes your foundations and leaves you feeling insecure. A disruption or interruption in your plans. A sudden change in scenery that will require going back to the drawing board. Sweeping change that will force you to adapt. A catastrophe or accident.

Reversed – Stability. Resistance to change. Things remaining the same. Feeling trapped in a rut or stuck in a situation. Inability to initiate change. Being unable to find a way out. Struggling to get access to something or someone. Not being able to get your voice heard.

The Star

Upright – A renewal of hope and optimism. Guidance and inspiration. Remaining faithful to your dreams and grander visions. Operating on faith. Staying the course. Encouragement. The attainment of your financial goals is on the horizon. Staying committed to what has been decided. Immunity to negative thoughts.

Reversed – Lacking direction. Feeling disillusioned or disappointed. Struggling to proceed. Questioning your direction. A loss of faith in your plans. Setbacks or delays when pursuing your financial goals. Getting sidetracked or distracted. Receiving confusing messages. Suffering from self-doubt. Confusion or disorganization. A need to rethink what you are doing.

The Moon

Upright – Uncertainty. Ambiguity. Things not appearing as they seem. A situation that is subject to change. Temporary. Murky conditions or confusion. Being unable to trust what you see. A need to go beneath the surface to find the truth. Falling prey to illusions or getting caught up in unrealistic dreams. A deal that is too good to be true.

Reversed – Getting overwhelmed by anxieties or fears that may not be rooted in reality. Emotional unrest or turmoil. Allowing your fears to lead your decision-making process. A lack of balance. Suppression of your intuition. Ignoring your gut. Things appearing worse than they are. A need to investigate.

The Sun

Upright – Attainment of your highest goals. Abundance. Prosperity. Success resulting from the fulfilment of your dreams. Feeling confident and on the right track. Examining things in the light of day. Liberation from commitments and debt. Financial success. Increased income. A windfall.

Reversed – A minor setback in your plans that is easily overcome. Partially achieving a goal or successfully taking the next step. A small stroke of luck. A temporary bad mood or passing feelings of negativity and doubt. Unexpected expenses. Temporary delays.

Judgement

Upright – Reawakening. Relinquishing the past. Turning over a new leaf. Establishing new habits. Starting over. Making important decisions about your finances. Evaluating your choices with clear vision. Figuring out what is really important to you. Deciding who your friends really are. Taking responsibility for your actions.

Reversed – Suffering from indecision. Being plagued by doubts. Dodging your responsibilities. Being unwilling to examine the circumstances of your life. Avoiding confrontation. Questioning if your financial plans are in accord with your values and beliefs. Delayed decisions. Not wanting to confront your fears.

The World

Upright – Completion. Fulfilment. Being made whole. Finding the missing pieces. Attaining an important milestone or accomplishing a major goal. Coming to the end of a journey. A new perspective. Gaining a deeper understanding of yourself and your finances. Abundance and financial stability. Prosperity. The fruits of your labour.

Reversed – Something remaining unfinished. Being in the middle of a process. Still growing and learning. Feeling out of sorts but being unable to understand why. A need to dig deeper and find out more. Experiencing limitations or restrictions on your behaviour or spending. Resisting change. Unable to reach completion or find closure.

PIPS AND COURT CARDS: FOCUSED MEANINGS

The pips and court cards provide significant information, but usually represent more focused, less all-encompassing influences on the situation when compared to the trump/Major Arcana cards. These cards fill in the details and help you understand all parts of a situation.

Wands

The Suit of Wands represents the fires of creation. This suit provides information about the forces that ignite your determination, push you to create and inspire you to take the lead. These cards illuminate your passions and show what gets you fired up and willing to act. They also help describe how you act under the pressure of success and failure. If a lot of Wands cards appear in a single reading, it means there is a lot of energy involved in the situation or a lot of new things are being initiated.

ACE OF WANDS

Upright – Inspiration. A new venture or business deal. Putting money into a new investment. Feeling enthusiastic about your prospects. Being driven to achieve. Seeking innovation or new approaches. Learning to incorporate your creativity into your financial planning. Scaling up. Taking a wider view or larger approach.

Reversed – A lack of energy. Feeling unmotivated. Struggling to stick to your plans. Difficulty brainstorming or finding solutions. Being stagnant or blocked. Attempts at creativity failing or taking longer to manifest than expected. Narrowing of focus. Possible tunnel vision. A cooling-down period. Risky or impulsive behaviours.

2 OF WANDS

Upright – Asserting control over your finances. Strategic planning. Reviewing your options. Making important decisions. Acting with authority. Breaking free from expectations or restraints so that you can do what you want. Long-term goals. A vision of the future. Ready to take advantage of opportunities that present themselves.

Reversed – Hesitation. Being unwilling to commit to a direction. Stuck between two options. Feeling out of control of your finances or overwhelmed by responsibility. Being unsure of the future. Getting stuck in a situation. Inability to wield your authority. Letting someone else take over and make decisions for you. A need to reestablish yourself.

3 OF WANDS

Upright – Having great foresight. Expanding your efforts or business. Reaping the rewards of past efforts. A solid foundation supporting your ventures. Work that is successfully underway. Putting things into action. Acting quickly. Negotiations and deals. Networking and influence. Travelling to further your interests.

Reversed – Not planning far enough in advance and therefore missing an opportunity. Being unready to take on a new challenge. Suffering from a lack of progress. Overconfidence leading to bad decisions. A flaw in your financial strategies. Not having enough patience to put your plans into action.

4 OF WANDS

Upright – Celebration. Recognition for your hard work. Acknowledgement of your achievements. Receiving positive attention. Basking in your successes. Accomplishing a significant goal. Help and support from others. Taking time to notice how far you have come. Financial security. A social safety net. An investment in time or money paying off.

Reversed – Achievements going unrecognized. A lack of support. Feeling ignored. Conflicts or disagreements with financial backers or partners. A difference in opinion about how to approach an issue. Disruptions to your income. Challenges to your decisions. Feelings of isolation or of being misunderstood.

5 OF WANDS

Upright – Competition. Conflicts or disagreements. Struggling to be heard. Dealing with people who don't have your goals or best interests in mind. Circular arguments or discussions that don't lead to a helpful resolution. Inability to jointly decide on an approach. Needing to defend your decisions. Remaining open to new strategies that will help you overcome obstacles.

Reversed – Disagreements beginning to be resolved. A decrease in tension. Overcoming challenges or obstacles. Agreeing to disagree. Finding common ground. Managing the expectations of others. Negotiating successfully. Meaningless challenges that won't actually affect your goals. A willingness to compromise. Harmony returning.

6 OF WANDS

Upright – Being on the verge of success. Beginning to see the results of your hard work. People noticing and reacting to your success. Others seeking your guidance on how to accomplish a goal. Taking time to acknowledge and celebrate what you have accomplished. Being in the public eye.

Reversed – A lack of validation. Fearing that your accomplishments don't amount to anything. Feeling stuck in endless effort. Losing faith in your overall goal and questioning if you are doing the right thing. Wavering commitment. Potentially being in it for the recognition and not for the actual goal at hand.

7 OF WANDS

Upright – Holding your own. Maintaining your position. Defending your opinions. Being at odds with others. Asserting yourself or establishing boundaries. Remaining steadfast and determined. Not giving up the fight. Competing with yourself or with others to win. Trying to remain on top.

Reversed – Being overwhelmed by your financial challenges. Fear that you can't keep going. Struggling to make people respect your boundaries. Feeling outnumbered or outvoted. Being affected by contrary opinions. Questioning yourself or suffering from a lack of confidence. Feeling like others are more prepared or capable than you.

8 OF WANDS

Upright – A rapid progression. Sudden developments. Feeling energized. Flash-in-the-pan opportunities. Being prepared to make a move at a moment's notice. Receiving news or an update that provides you with new financial possibilities. Several things happening at one time. Remaining aware and adaptable. Putting your plans into action. Setting things into motion.

Reversed – A slow-down. Unexpected delays. Investments or other efforts not developing as quickly as you would like. A lack of direction or a path that is blocked. Misunderstandings. Unclear communications. Missed opportunities. Suspended efforts. Abandoning a course of action. Indecisiveness.

9 OF WANDS

Upright – A work in progress. Being in the middle of things. Experience that leads to understanding. Hope and determination. A momentary rest but a willingness to get back to work. Perseverance. Strength of character. Understanding how to cope with setbacks or obstacles. Staying vigilant even when things are going well.

Reversed – Feeling exhausted or overcome. Experiencing burnout due to financial pressures or obligations. Questioning the cost of your plans and the validity of your efforts. Feeling insecure about your decisions and your ability to defend them. Doubting your own actions. Feeling bombarded.

10 OF WANDS

Upright – Shouldering a burden. Putting your head down and getting to work. Bearing the brunt of your decisions. Committing yourself or obligating yourself to someone or something. Managing several different things at once. Taking on more than you can handle. Needing to review your priorities. Trying to be all things for all people.

Reversed – Being released from an obligation. Liberation. Assessing your burdens and deciding which ones you really need to carry. A lightening of your load. Refocusing on what is important. The end of a commitment. Letting go of ideas, beliefs or actions that no longer help you get what you want. Delegating your responsibilities.

PAGE OF WANDS

Upright – Exploration and discovery. Finding out something new. Feeling enthusiastic. Wanting to go on an adventure. Being willing to take risks and make bold moves. Making spontaneous but inspired decisions. Taking a creative approach to your financial decisions. A time of experimentation. Testing a new theory.

Reversed – Being closed off from new experiences. A lack of direction or focus. Feeling unmotivated. Struggling to summon up the energy to enact your plans. Aimlessness or restlessness. Suffering from stagnation or a lack of new ideas. A loss of passion or enthusiasm for what you are doing.

KNIGHT OF WANDS

Upright – Dynamic action. Acting without hesitation. Embracing challenges. Channelling your passion into your efforts. Acting from a sense of purpose or being inspired by an ideal. A desire to grow or expand. A tendency to innovate and initiate action. Being comfortable with change and the evolution of your financial plans.

Reversed – Being reckless or feeling impatient. Wanting everything now. Being unwilling to wait for your efforts to come to fruition. Rushing into a situation without thinking about the consequences. A tendency toward overconfidence. Getting in too deep. Overinvesting your time or money in something. A lack of proportion.

QUEEN OF WANDS

Upright – Confidence. Taking the lead. Using your passion and enthusiasm to inspire others. Allowing your charisma to shine through. Networking. Asking for and granting favours. Being an instigator and leveraging your influence. Asserting yourself. Clearly stating your expectations. Holding others accountable. Being passionate about your work.

Reversed – A hesitation to take the lead. Self-doubt creeping in and causing you to lose confidence. An inability to speak up or clearly communicate your needs. Not being sure if you are up to a task. Feeling disempowered. Conversely, fear or uncertainty leading to being too controlling. Micromanaging. Leaving nothing to chance.

KING OF WANDS

Upright – A strong and reliable vision for the future. Sensible and actionable ideas about how to advance your fortunes. Wielding your influence to get what you want. Taking charge of your financial fate and arranging things to your liking. An entrepreneurial spirit. Successful launch of a business venture.

Reversed – An unsure leader. Someone who doesn't know what they are talking about. Procrastination and hesitation. Lack of knowledge and inability to admit it. Difficulty figuring out what your goals should be. Not being sure of the details. Overconfidence leading to future problems. Wagers or taking a badly thought-out risk.

Cups

The Suit of Cups symbolizes the watery repositories of our emotions and intuitive powers. These cards provide insight into the hidden currents that move you emotionally. They help illustrate what is going on in your soul and subconscious mind. The Cups also provide insight into the health of your relationships and how easily you express your feelings. Several Cups appearing in a reading point to an emotionally overwhelming situation or one that requires intuition and wisdom to navigate.

ACE OF CUPS

Upright – Emotional renewal. Getting a fresh start. Positive emotions. Inner peace. Committing yourself to a cause or ideal. Receiving emotional satisfaction from your job. Working in a spiritual setting. Your work aligning with your emotions or spiritual beliefs. An emotional bond with someone that may impact your finances.

Reversed – Inner turmoil. Feeling unsettled. Not feeling at home in your workplace or place of business. A lack of joy in your work. Emotional conflicts that make work difficult or negatively impact your finances. Repressing your emotions or denying how you feel. A boss that doesn't take your needs into consideration.

ACE of CUPS.

2 OF CUPS

Upright – Harmonious partnership. Getting the support you need or supporting someone. Collaboration that leads to a positive financial outcome. Mutually beneficial partnership. Getting along with your coworkers. Sharing similar values with a coworker or client. Working together to achieve success.

Reversed – Difficult professional relationships. Disagreeing with a partner about how to manage your money. Lack of support at home or in the workplace. Difficulty communicating financial needs or coming to a consensus. A need to renegotiate contracts or revisit agreements.

3 OF CUPS

Upright – A celebration. Taking time to recognize how far you have come and what you have accomplished. Taking a break to indulge in pleasurable activities. A supportive work environment with people who genuinely want to see you succeed. Leveraging social connections to further your career goals or financial initiatives.

Reversed – A joyless time. Feeling overburdened and unable to enjoy your life. Poor work/life balance. A difficult work environment that is not supportive. Isolating yourself instead of making connections and growing your network. Feeling like you don't have anyone to confide in. Inability to enjoy the fruits of your labour.

THE GOLDEN GRIMOIRE

4 OF CUPS

Upright – Dissatisfaction. Being unsure of your purpose. A desire to focus on and better understand your emotions. Taking time out to rethink your goals and your approach to financial success. Possible tunnel vision. Not seeing all the possible options.

Reversed – A breakthrough or sudden realization. Moving out of a time of contemplation and into action. Taking a renewed interest in your money or career. Being aware of options and possibilities. Rethinking options you previously disregarded. Turning over a new leaf.

5 OF CUPS

Upright – A disappointment. Experiencing a setback. Plans going awry. A lack of success. Dealing with the emotional fallout of failure. Focusing on what went wrong. Potentially learning from your mistakes. Not being aware of what is working in your favour.

Reversed – Turning things around. Leaving disappointments in the past. Refocusing your energy on the future. Shedding old perspectives. Forgiving yourself or others. Turning a defeat into a victory. Starting to look forward to what is coming next.

6 OF CUPS

Upright – Having an appreciation for the past. Feeling nostalgic. Getting inspiration from previous experiences. Giving or receiving a thoughtful gift. Reconnecting with someone from your past who could help you with your business or financial goals. Being proud of where you have come from or what you have overcome.

Reversed – Wrestling with beliefs or experiences from your past. Feeling limited by previous experiences. Relying on an outdated approach. Working with old information. A bad influence from your past. Resting on the laurels of past achievements for too long.

7 OF CUPS

Upright – Abundant possibilities. A variety of choices. Potentially being spoiled for choice. Lack of clarity. A need for careful consideration and decision-making. Potentially not fully understanding the ramifications of your choice. Bad opportunities masquerading as good opportunities. Getting caught up with fantasies but not doing the work.

Reversed – Being focused and practical. Underwhelming choices. Realistic goals but potential lack of vision. Clarity after confusion. Eliminating choices to simplify your decision-making process. Identifying achievable and positive goals. Resisting temptation.

8 OF CUPS

Upright – Leaving an emotionally burdensome situation. Seeking a job that fulfils you emotionally and spiritually. An adjustment in your career path. Reassessing your desires and needs and tailoring your financial plan to support them. Choosing to challenge yourself rather than take the easy road.

Reversed – Holding onto a job that no longer serves your purposes. Clinging to people who don't have your best interests at heart. Resisting necessary changes. Remaining in a difficult situation. Repeatedly dealing with problems rather than seeking solutions. Feeling emotionally or mentally underequipped to deal with your situation.

9 OF CUPS

Upright – Profound satisfaction. Achieving your goals and appreciating what you have. Getting what you have wished and worked for. Being on the path to success and reaping the rewards. Seeing the fruits of your labour. Being able to enjoy and savour your accomplishments.

Reversed – A minor and temporary setback. A problem that may appear worse than it really is. A trifling challenge that will not require much effort to overcome. Getting what you want, but the achievement taking slightly longer than you planned. An eventual happy ending.

10 OF CUPS

Upright – A fulfilling and satisfactory career. A harmonious life. Contentment. Feeling in tune with your values. Having all that you need, practically and emotionally. Emotional fulfilment through your career. Joyful abundance.

Reversed – Feeling that something isn't right. A disharmony or a feeling that something is out of place. A need to check the details and make sure you know what is happening with your finances. Someone who isn't being honest with you or who has ulterior motives. Disruptions in your personal lifestyle or work life.

PAGE OF CUPS

Upright – Allowing your emotions to inspire your decision-making process. Taking a creative and intuitive approach to solving problems. Being open to innovative ideas. Noticing and interpreting emotional signals from others. Beginning to feel emotional satisfaction but understanding there is more to do.

Reversed – Being either overly expressive or emotionally closed off. Feeling as though you can't fully be yourself professionally. Struggling with idealistic notions. Retreating into daydreams or fantasy rather than confronting reality. Not backing up what you intuit with facts.

KNIGHT OF CUPS

Upright – Turning your career into a grand and romantic adventure. Feeling driven by your ideals or a primary goal. Feeling committed to achieving your dreams. Being willing to work on behalf of others. Taking emotional risks to accomplish your goals.

Reversed – A warning that you might be acting too freely or impulsively. Overwhelming enthusiasm that sweeps you away. Jumping in without looking. Assuming everyone else is as willing as you are to take risks. Following your bliss.

QUEEN OF CUPS

Upright – Navigating emotional situations with grace and empathy. Taking care of others' feelings. Creating a safe place for people to express themselves. Fostering understanding. Being clear when expressing your emotional needs and expectations. Making decisions compassionately.

Reversed – Struggling to connect with people emotionally. Feeling distant or isolated. Not understanding how others perceive you. Being unwilling or unable to care for others emotionally. Being "all business". Refusing to be swayed emotionally. Having an iron grip on your emotions.

KING OF CUPS

Upright – Being an emotional, compassionate and understanding leader. Having a healthy understanding of your emotional reactions. Putting your emotions to work for you. Using your feelings to drive your efforts. Ensuring the emotional wellbeing of yourself and others.

Reversed – Being emotionally out of balance. Struggling to reconcile your feelings and reality. Avoiding responsibility for your actions. Being unable to clearly express your emotions. Leaning on others for support even if you don't need it.

Swords

The Suit of Swords symbolizes the airy, sweeping and penetrative power of the mind. The Swords provide information about how a situation is being addressed intellectually. The Swords reveal your deepest and most hidden thoughts. They show you how clearly you are thinking and if the channels of communication are clear or cluttered. If there are a lot of Swords in a reading, it can indicate argument, conversations and debate or confused thoughts.

ACE OF SWORDS

Upright – Mental rejuvenation. Having a breakthrough or sudden realization. Mental clarity and logical thinking. Initiation of a plan or process. Innovation. Reduction of confusion. A captivating and stimulating new idea. Inspiration. Ambition tempered by logic and careful thought.

Reversed – Lack of clarity. Misunderstanding. Confused or garbled communication. Rejection of logic or facts. A lack of information that causes uncertainty. Making an uninformed or snap decision. Defying logic. Taking things at face value. Allowing your emotions to lead when you should be thinking things through.

2 OF SWORDS

Upright – A still point. A moment of indecision or deliberation. A stalemate or equally balanced forces. Striking a balance between conflicting requirements. A crossroads or place of decision. An end to conflict or conversation. A waiting period. Choosing between two equally important things, such as two job offers.

Reversed – Delaying or avoiding a decision. Putting your head in the sand. Refusing to seek more information. Not confronting a challenging situation. Unresolved conflicts with partners or coworkers. Refusing to face facts. Indecision. Delays. Inability to act.

3 OF SWORDS

Upright – Financial losses resulting from an emotional upheaval. The need to deal with a setback. The time needed to process a disappointment. A job loss or demotion. An extreme workplace conflict. Disillusionment with your career. Struggling to come to terms with a situation.

Reversed – Recovering from a financial loss. Moving past a difficulty and getting on with your life. Resolving a dispute or disagreement. The growth that comes from adversity. Starting to heal from a disappointment. Renewal of faith. Rediscovering your inner strength.

4 OF SWORDS

Upright – Taking a break. A vacation or pause in your work life. Delegation of tasks. Asking someone for assistance. Potentially a period of sickness and a need for recuperation. A time for strategic planning. A corporate retreat. Approaching investments with caution.

Reversed – Feeling rejuvenated. Knowing exactly what you want to do. Pushing yourself to achieve. Consolidating your power. Putting on an impressive show. Possibly burning the candle at both ends. The energy that follows a forced period of inactivity.

5 OF SWORDS

Upright – A conflict or confrontation. Disagreements with partners or coworkers. A lack of support for your choices. Someone actively working against you. Risky or unethical financial practices. Untrustworthy behaviour. Power struggles. Needing to stand up for yourself.

Reversed – A reduction in tensions. Coming to an agreement or understanding. Recovery from losses. Escaping a difficult situation. Winning a court case. Successful mediation. A cooperative workplace or boss. Teamwork. Trying to act in harmony with others.

6 OF SWORDS

Upright – Moving away from a difficult situation and into a better one. Better options becoming available. Leaving behind financial troubles or an unhappy workplace. Discovering a solution to your problems. A job opportunity or raise. Remaining open to possibilities.

Reversed – Being unable to escape a difficult situation. Feeling stuck in your career. Deciding to remain where you are in an effort to improve the situation. Accepting and facing difficulties. Unexpected expenses or setbacks. Weathering the storm.

7 OF SWORDS

Upright – Deception. The potential of betrayal. Untrustworthy associates. Someone is lying to you. Proceed with caution. Being careful when signing contracts or making agreements. Being conservative and careful with your finances and resources. Vetting someone carefully before you trust them.

Reversed – Secrets or dishonesty revealed. Seeing things how they really are. Discovering a hidden agenda or plan. Seeing through someone's lies. Being honest and upfront about your intentions and goals. Revealing the truth. Consequences. Acting with integrity. Rebuilding trust.

8 OF SWORDS

Upright – Obstruction. Restriction. Feeling hemmed in or forced into a situation. Entrapment. Financial obligations that must be confronted before you can make progress. Possibly being willingly blind to options. Refusing to see the truth. A dead-end job. An unfulfilling career.

Reversed – Release. A feeling of liberation. Escaping from a trap. Seeing beyond self-imposed limitations. Finding a new way forward. Leaving behind fears or uncertainties. Feeling a new sense of abundance and growth. Breathing new life into your career or business.

9 OF SWORDS

Upright – Anxiety. Worries and concerns. Feeling at risk. Uncertainty. Losing sleep over finances or work issues. Work-related stress. Overthinking. Being a victim of your own thoughts. Being overwhelmed by obligations. Forgetting to take care of yourself. Destructive thoughts.

Reversed – Emotional recovery. A reduction in stress. Increased peace of mind when it comes to your finances or budget. Developing a positive mindset despite setbacks or worries. Self-confidence. Handling work stress in a healthy way. Developing inner strength.

10 OF SWORDS

Upright – Something coming to an end. A financial or professional setback or defeat. Loss of a job or failure of a business venture. Potential bankruptcy or monetary losses. Failed investments. A project ending poorly. Unsuccessful effort. A challenging time that opens up new opportunities.

Reversed – The end of a cycle. Recovery and renewal after financial difficulties. Overcoming setbacks and defeats. Turning a defeat into an eventual victory. Escaping something that has been causing you difficulties for a long time. Learning from past experiences.

PAGE OF SWORDS

Upright – Feelings of curiosity. Being open to new experiences. A desire to learn new things. Figuring out how to make yourself heard. Being proactive and inquisitive when making financial choices. Seeking creative solutions to your needs. Observing how others innovate and learning from it.

Reversed – Thinking you know it all. Not being willing to watch and learn. Impatience with how other people do things. Being unwilling to change your mind. Impulsivity. Lack of caution when making decisions.

KNIGHT OF SWORDS

Upright – Fast and focused action. Determination. Being willing to strike out boldly. Wielding your mind like a weapon. Not backing down from an intellectual challenge. Aggressively seeking out information. Being ready and willing to act at a moment's notice.

Reversed – Being reckless. Moving too quickly. Events that are out of control. Not being able to control the narrative. Starting something you can't finish. Biting off more than you can chew. Failing to make adequate plans. Rushing in before you are ready.

QUEEN OF SWORDS

Upright – Supreme clarity of thought. Seeing past masks and misrepresentations. A sharp intellect that can quickly and easily organize and understand information. Using logic to plan your decisions and plot your path. Taking an important leadership position. Managing resources well.

Reversed – Excessive criticism. Being sceptical of everything. Someone who is closed off or unwilling to entertain new ideas. Picking apart decisions. Difficulty communicating. Appearing cold or uncaring. Being closed off from opportunities or other people.

Upright – Control and authority over your financial decisions. Gaining autonomy. Finding financial freedom. Making sound choices and helping others to do the same. Leading by example. Teaching others. Using strategy, logic and data to plan your future. Empowerment and strength.

Reversed – Wielding too much authority. Throwing your weight around. Pushing people to do what you want. Creating conflict or an oppositional relationship. Being unwilling to listen to suggestions or alternative solutions. Refusal to collaborate. Not taking good advice.

Pentacles

The Suit of Pentacles represents the earthy building blocks of creation. This suit informs you about the physical, material elements that are influencing you. Pentacles inform you about your health, your finances and your surroundings. They provide information about how you handle practical situations and responsibilities. If there are a lot of Pentacles in a reading, it could mean the situation is bogged down and evolving slowly or that a lot of financial dealings are in play.

ACE OF PENTACLES

Upright – The seed of prosperity and wealth. A good time to invest in your future. Being at the beginning of your financial journey. New financial opportunities. A new job or position in your company. Starting a new business. A fresh start. A period of renewed stability.

Reversed – Improper handling of money or resources. Poor planning. Reduction in stability. Risky spending behaviours. Financial uncertainties. Difficulties in the workplace. Being passed over for a promotion. Trouble finding a job. A financial dead end.

2 OF PENTACLES

Upright – Striking a dynamic balance between your income and your expenses. Managing your responsibilities with skill and grace. Maintaining awareness of your responsibilities. Expending effort to make things work. An adaptable financial plan. Handling more than one job or income stream.

Reversed – An imbalance in your income versus your expenses. Being in debt. Struggling to follow your financial plan. Daily responsibilities interfering with your ability to save. Neglecting one set of responsibilities to manage another. A budget you can't maintain. Overwhelming workload.

3 OF PENTACLES

Upright – Uniting with others to accomplish a goal. Contributing your expertise to a group effort. Consulting with experts for guidance. Initiating a joint venture. A new team project. Building your skills. Being respected in your field.

Reversed – Difficulties working with others. Conflicting viewpoints. Lack of teamwork. Bad advice or incorrect information. A difficult work environment. A project that is not going as planned. Unsuccessful collaboration. Imbalanced work relationships. Possible struggles with authority.

4 OF PENTACLES

Upright – Financial control. Stability. Maintenance and care of your resources. Feeling secure. Careful and cautious investments. Being averse to risk-taking. Holding on tightly to the familiar. Sticking with what you know. A need to maintain control over yourself and your situation.

Reversed – Sudden instability or a surprising change. Feeling unsure of your current situation or prospects. Fears of losing it all. Greed, hoarding or unproductive investing. Holding onto material possessions. Financial stagnation or lack of progress. Frantic acts to rebuild what you had.

5 OF PENTACLES

Upright – Financial difficulties. A great material loss. A struggle for survival. Poverty or homelessness. Job loss. Food insecurity. A reduction of pay or income. Difficulties making ends meet. Unexpected bills or expenses. Heavy financial burdens. Feelings of isolation.

Reversed – A gradual improvement to your situation. The reduction of work-related challenges. Finding a solution to your problems. Starting to see the light at the end of the tunnel. A rebirth of hope. Assistance from others. Exploring an alternative solution. Beginning to rebuild.

6 OF PENTACLES

Upright – An equitable exchange of resources. Generosity of spirit. Charity work. Receiving or giving assistance. Sharing your knowledge and skills with others. Mentorship. Being paid what you are worth. Unexpectedly receiving money. A blessing. A lucky break. Sharing the wealth. A good time to invest.

Reversed – Exploitation or uneven distribution of proceeds. Unequal treatment. Misuse of power. Favouritism in the workplace. Not getting paid in full. Debt. Misuse of money or misdirection of funds. Failed investments. Lack of assistance. An unexpected loss.

THE GOLDEN GRIMOIRE

7 OF PENTACLES

Upright – Assessment and evaluation. Patience. Reviewing the facts. Assessing the results. Being willing to wait to see the results of your efforts. Slow growth. Rethinking your career path. Annual financial review. Readjusting or fine-tuning your future plans. Being persistent but willing to adapt.

Reversed – Lack of patience. Not seeing enough progress. Being unsatisfied with your career or business. Making hasty or poorly thought-out decisions. Not seeing the fruits of your labour or being blind to them. Feelings of frustration.

8 OF PENTACLES

Upright – Artistry. Dedication. A job well done. Mastery. Handling your investments, job or business with the utmost care. Hard work and persistence. A deep focus on your job. Using all your skills to get the job done. A work of art. Following your budget with exacting care.

Reversed – Distraction. Lack of focus. Unwillingness to commit. A reduction in motivation. Feeling dispirited about your financial prospects. Unfulfilling work. Going through the motions. Complacency. Not paying attention to details. Lack of follow-through.

9 OF PENTACLES

Upright – Financial independence. Luxury. Being self-sufficient. Great prosperity. Abundant resources. Enjoying what you have worked for. Professional achievement and recognition. Possibly a professional reward. Experiencing the results of a healthy and functioning budget. Relaxation and fulfilment.

Reversed – Crumbling financial dependence. Feeling anxious about your money, job or career. Dissatisfaction with your job. Feeling you are experiencing undeserved bad luck. Looking to others for validation. Ill-advised pursuit of luxury. Overspending. Not following your budget.

10 OF PENTACLES

Upright – The pot of gold at the end of the rainbow. Long-term financial success and stability. Generational wealth. A solid foundation for your life and your family. The pinnacle of your career or potentially a happy retirement. The culmination of all your hard work. Accumulated wealth. Inheritance.

Reversed – Difficulty securing your future. An event that derails your financial plans. Relying too heavily on one stream of income. Failed investments. A monetary loss late in life. The need to protect your belongings and investments. Financial plans that aren't in alignment with family values.

PAGE OF PENTACLES

Upright – The beginning of a journey. Diligence. A focus on learning new skills or making progress on a new goal. The potential for success with continued effort. An apprenticeship, an internship or just starting out. Learning the ropes. Beginning to invest.

Reversed – Frivolity. Lack of discipline. Feeling directionless. Missing out on chances to learn or grow new skills. Struggling to find your footing at a new job. Feeling overwhelmed and unable to make progress. Emotional overspending. Inability to control yourself.

KNIGHT OF PENTACLES

Upright – Reliability. Hard work. Someone who is dependable. Being open to hard work. Strategically planning for your career and future financial stability. Commitment to success. Looking to the future while remaining rooted in the present. A desire for methodical progress.

Reversed – Flightiness. Lack of progress in your career. An unwillingness to commit. Difficulty making progress. Inertia. Looking to the horizon and not seeing what is right in front of you. Financial stagnation or mismanagement. Depletion of your nest egg.

QUEEN OF PENTACLES

Upright – Financial wisdom. Careful nurturing of your financial prospects. Someone who is grounded and resourceful. Practicality. The ability to nurture projects and see them through to fruition. Someone willing to mentor others or provide guidance.

Reversed – Not taking care of your financial obligations. Being unwilling to take responsibility for your money or career. Overdependence on someone else for your success. Being focused only on money and material wealth. Either an unwillingness to help others or a tendency to get taken advantage of.

KING OF PENTACLES

Upright – Financial authority. Knowing what you want and how to get it. Making rational and practical plans for the future. Career success. Prosperity and accomplishment. Being skilled at business. The ability to lead and direct others. Smart investments. Leading others to success.

Reversed – An inability to assert your authority or a tendency to overpower others. Forcing others to comply with your wishes. Being aggressive in your career or investments. Focusing too much on material success. Greed. Speculation.

CRAFTING A PERSONAL PROSPERITY SIGIL

Though it may sound counterintuitive, magical tools you create yourself will always be more powerful than anything you can buy. It will always be fun and rewarding to search metaphysical stores and thrift stores for spell components like boxes, incense and oils, but the magic you make with items you handcraft will be imbued with an extra dose of power that you can't get anywhere else. When I tell people this, they are often sceptical. If they are new to magic or inexperienced with the required techniques, how can they make a powerful tool? The secret lies within the fact that anything you make will be more deeply attuned to yourself and your needs. Even if the tool doesn't look as impressive as one you can buy, it will be easier to use and it will mesh seamlessly with your intentions and desires. It's the difference between buying something off the rack and custom-making it for yourself. It is just going to fit better.

This chapter will be an in-depth explanation of how to make a personal prosperity sigil. Unlike other sigils that are usually made for a single purpose, charged with magical power and then destroyed, this sigil is something you will continue to use over time. The more you use it, the more powerful it will become. It will absorb the full range of your intentions and ideas about what it means to be truly prosperous and help to support you in your efforts when you are performing money, wealth and prosperity magic. As your relationship with this symbol grows, you will discover that it can help you while you are making important decisions and act as a guide in your daily life.

As mentioned previously in this book, your financial goals will change based on your current needs and your personal vision of prosperity. If you are in the middle of a financial crisis, you will not be performing the same magical workings you would be if you were about to launch a small business. A personal prosperity sigil can be used at any point in your journey and in conjunction with any other form of magic.

This sigil can accompany you on your journey to prosperity from start to finish, because you don't need a lot of materials to make it. All you need is paper, something to write with and some time.

BACKGROUND INFORMATION

What are sigils?

The word "sigil" comes from the Latin word *sigillum*, which means sign. In modern magical terms, it is a simplified symbol that is used to assist in the manifestation of your intent. There are many different ways to create them, but this chapter will focus on a method specific to creating a prosperity sigil.

How are sigils used in magic?

Sigils are representations of a desired outcome or state of being. The process of their creation is a way to tap into the subconscious and evoke the imagery and ideas that will help achieve a goal. After their creation, they are charged with magical power. Usually, the sigil is then ceremoniously destroyed. The destruction of the sigil releases all the pent-up magical power, which is then dispersed into the universe to do the bidding of the magician. However, there are other ways to use sigils that don't incorporate their destruction. They can be used as meditation tools or left in a place to slowly release the influence they embody.

The prosperity sigil described in this chapter is not meant to be destroyed (although you can certainly deploy it in this way if you choose). It is meant to be used repeatedly so that it is strengthened and perpetually imbued with additional magical intent. The more you work with the image, the more powerful it will become. It will be a great ally in achieving your financial goals and assuring your continued prosperity.

The purpose of a personal prosperity sigil

This sigil is a magical design that acts as a holistic summary of all your intentions for your wealth, financial stability and prosperity. It is a living symbol that will connect your innermost desires with the furthest reaches of the universe and bring them to fruition. Incorporating this symbol into your daily life and magical practices will help you create, maintain and sustain your prosperity while sheltering you from events that could negatively impact your wealth.

The personal prosperity sigil is designed to be multifunctional. If you put careful thought and sustained effort into creating it, it will encompass all the facets of life that touch upon and have an influence on your financial stability. It will attract prosperous influences and events and disperse them appropriately. It will help defend you from financial mishaps and bad habits like impulse spending. And it will help clarify your thinking when you are making plans for your prosperous future.

What's the catch?

At this point, you might find yourself wondering about the downside. A powerful magical tool that can be made with a small number of inexpensive resources that are easy to obtain? One that will help you sustain a prosperous state of being while adapting to your every need and protecting you from some of the pitfalls you might experience while stabilizing your financial health? Is it too good to be true?

It isn't too good to be true, but in addition to requiring paper and something to write with, the creation of this sigil requires time and effort on your part. I am not going to sugarcoat it. It takes ten days to make the personal prosperity sigil. The process is not difficult, but it might seem a little complex at first. Dare to commit yourself to this process even if you feel a little unsure about how it will go. This tool isn't a quick fix, but it is reliable. And the more time and attention you dedicate to making it, the more powerful it will be from the very start.

You might be wondering why you can't create the sigil all in one day.

You can if you choose. In fact, you could sit down right now, sketch out a simple design, and start putting it to use immediately. But there are three primary benefits to using the full ten days to perfect your magical creation.

First, when you work magic, you are engaging in a conversation not just with the universe but with your inner self. The most successful magic sets up a channel of communication between yourself and the universe to facilitate the desired results. The energy and effort you put into your magic travels in two different directions – out into the world at large, and inwards to the very centre of your being. In both cases repetition, layering symbolism, creating variations on a theme and establishing routines help to build that channel and improve your chances of success. When it comes to the creation of a magical tool you intend to use for a long time, these concepts are doubly important.

Second, it is important to acknowledge all the different kinds of energy that fuel your magical work. The effort it takes to prepare for a spell – for example, finding the perfect supplies and calculating the right time – is not lost. It becomes a part of the overall energy that is channelled toward the desired intent. If you choose to embark on a ten-day magical process, you might experience a variety of emotions. You could feel a rush of anticipation because you are looking forward to the end results. Frustration could overwhelm you because you really would prefer to do it all at once and just get it over with. Or anxiety may creep up on you because you are afraid you will forget and accidentally skip a day. All the energy generated by these feelings gets channelled into the work itself. The narrower a stream of water is, the more powerful its flow. The more you accept limitations and requirements as part of your magical process, the more powerful it will be.

Third, the structure of this work is based on the seven classical planets, and each day is used as a gateway for accessing their characteristic powers (*see* "Planetary Meditations/Reflections" on page 126). If you create your personal prosperity sigil over the course of ten days, you will be able to infuse it with the planetary energy that rules each day of the week.

General ideas for using this sigil

Once you have created your sigil, it can be used in every single spell or ritual in this book and in any other spell or ritual you perform to increase your prosperity and wealth. However, it can also be used on its own.

Here are some examples of ways you could use the sigil alone:

- Take a picture of it and use it as your phone or computer wallpaper so you see it every day.
- Carry a copy of it in your wallet or purse.
- Draw it on the side of a plant pot and grow a hearty plant such as a fern in it, to associate the growth of the plant with the growth of your wealth.
- Trace it on your front and back door or the door of your room to draw wealth.

A final note before we start

At this point, I feel like I must make clear that you don't have to "know how to draw" or "be artistic" or "crafty" to make yourself a personal prosperity sigil (in fact, the instructions below include some tips for people who aren't used to drawing). The goal is to come up with a design that is simple and easy to visualize. If you can make marks on paper, you can do this! You are a magician capable of wielding the powers of the universe. So don't get daunted by false ideas about your limitations.

CREATING YOUR SIGIL

Intention-setting

It shouldn't be a surprise that before you create a sigil to reshape your life, you need to know what you want your future life to look like. Refer to the previous chapter for information on how to define and understand your personal vision of prosperity. You don't need to know all the details of this envisioned future. In fact, the process of creating the sigil will help you fill in the fine details and get a better understanding of what prosperity means to you. However, throughout this work, you must be able to envision yourself in a general state of prosperity. You should know what it looks like and, more importantly, what it feels like. Take your time and make sure the image and feeling are fixed firmly in your mind before you begin.

Supplies

There are only two supplies you absolutely need to complete this work:

- Paper (unlined or lined, it doesn't matter)
- A pen or pencil

Here are some other supplies you may wish to use but which aren't required:

- Candles (green or gold) and a sturdy candleholder for each
- Magical liquid for blessing (olive oil, magical oil, holy water or perfume of your choice)
- A number of small sticks (such as wooden matchsticks, skewers, pick-up sticks or twigs), if you want to use them to help inspire your sigil design
- An image or representation of an entity, if you would like to call upon their aid/blessing during the construction of the sigil

Notes

- Read through the entire set of instructions before you start so you know what to expect.
- The information below is a framework that you can customize to fit your personality, beliefs and lifestyle. I will include information about using candles and working with a spiritual ally like an ancestor, god or other entity, but these are suggestions.
- Start your work on a Friday.
- You may wish to do this work while the moon is waxing (getting bigger) in the sky, but it is not required.
- You may wish to do this work at the same time every day (for example, as soon as you wake up, at sunset or before bed), but it is not required.
- You may wish to ground and centre yourself before each day's work. *See* the Appendix (page 298) for more information.

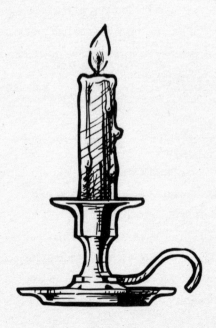

Day 1 — Friday

GOAL – PAPER PREPARATION

The goal of this day is:

🔥 To prepare the paper on which you will create your personal prosperity sigil.

1. Begin by doing something to set the mood and let your subconscious mind and inner self know it is time to work magic. You may choose to do one or more of the following:
    - 🔥 Light a candle and/or incense
    - 🔥 Call upon the aid or presence of an entity to oversee what you are doing
    - 🔥 Ground and centre yourself
    - 🔥 Spend a few moments in quiet contemplation

2. You will bless two pages of paper. Do this step for each page. Touch each corner of the paper while saying, "Blessed be this paper so that it may assist me in my magical work." You can do this with your bare finger, or you can anoint each corner with a magical liquid.

3. Bless a pen or pencil by holding it and saying, "Blessed be this tool so that it may assist me in my magical work." You can do this with your bare hands, or you can rub a small amount of a magical liquid on your pen or pencil.

FOUNDATIONS OF FINANCIAL MAGIC

4. Using the pen or pencil you just blessed, divide one of the sheets of paper into seven rows (we will call this page 1). The rows don't have to be perfect or evenly spaced, but you should have enough space to doodle or sketch in them. Using the names of the planets or planetary glyphs, label each row in this order:
- 🜂 Saturn (♄)
- 🜂 Sun (☉)
- 🜂 Moon (☽)
- 🜂 Mars (♂)
- 🜂 Mercury (☿)
- 🜂 Jupiter (♃)
- 🜂 Venus (♀)

5. After dividing page 1 into seven rows, divide it into two columns. Again, the columns don't have to be perfect, but you should have room to doodle or sketch in each box. Label the left-hand column with your full name, or your magical name if you have one. Label the right-hand column with the words "Perpetual Prosperity".

6. Page 2 should remain blank for now.

7. Carefully store both pages and your pencil or pen in a place where no one else will see or touch them. You can fold the paper if you need to, or you can even keep it between the pages of a book. Just remember that if you have used oil or water to bless the paper it could stain the inside of a book, so use caution.

THE GOLDEN GRIMOIRE

Full or Magickal Name	PERPETUAL PROSPERITY
♄ SATURN	
☉ SUN	
☽ MOON	
♂ MARS	
☿ MERCURY	
♃ JUPITER	
♀ VENUS	

FOUNDATIONS OF FINANCIAL MAGIC

Day 2 — Saturday

GOAL – SATURN MEDITATION/CREATION OF TWO SATURN SIGILS

The goals of this day are:

- To meditate on Saturn's planetary power and how it can influence and support your personal behaviour, financial behaviour and ideas about prosperity.
- To sketch a small design or doodle that represents the attributes of Saturn you want to embody so that you are financially successful.
- To sketch a small design or doodle that represents the Saturnian influences that contribute to living in a state of perpetual prosperity.

1. Begin by doing something to set the mood and let your subconscious mind and inner self know it is time to work magic. You may choose to do one or more of the following:
   - Light a candle and/or incense
   - Call upon the aid or presence of an entity to oversee what you are doing
   - Ground and centre yourself
   - Spend a few moments in quiet contemplation

2. Retrieve page 1 and your pencil/pen from wherever you stored them. Place them in front of you.

3. While visualizing what perpetual prosperity looks like for you, say, "Powers of Saturn, infuse me with your wisdom and lead me deeper into understanding. Show me the way to perpetual prosperity."

4. Read the reflection on Saturn's contribution to perpetual prosperity and financial success, on page 126.
   - Spend some time meditating on these concepts and any others that come to mind. Allow yourself to be open to any thoughts that float into your head (if they don't seem to be related to Saturn, just allow them to float back out – but don't be too quick to dismiss them, because they could be there to give you important information).
   - Once you have finished meditating, it's time to sketch a doodle

or design in the Saturn row of each column. Neither shape should be elaborate or overly detailed. If you get stuck on what to draw, throw some small sticks onto your table and gaze at the shapes they make. Allow yourself to casually sketch something in each column of the Saturn row – one to represent the attributes of Saturn you wish to embody (in the column under your name), and one to represent the planet's influence on perpetual prosperity (in the Personal Prosperity column).

- If you are unable to come up with anything to draw, remember that your sketch can be as simple as a single curved or straight line. To represent the idea of barriers or restrictions, you could draw something as concrete as a wall or as abstract as a small, tight circle. If you intuit Saturn means limiting your spending so you can save more money, you could draw a bag of money with a lock on it or a dollar sign in a box.

- Now here is the downright difficult part. The moment you are done sketching, put the paper away. Don't look at the images, don't review them, don't revise them. Just put the paper and pen away and extinguish the candle.

Days 3–8 — Sunday, Monday, Tuesday, Wednesday, Thursday and Friday

The goals of each day are:

🔥 To meditate on each day's planetary power and how it can influence and support your personal behaviour, financial behaviour and ideas about prosperity.

🔥 To sketch a small design or doodle that represents attributes of the day's planet you want to embody so that you are financially successful.

🔥 To sketch a small design or doodle that represents the influences of the day's planet that contribute to living in a state of perpetual prosperity.

1. Begin by doing something to set the mood and let your subconscious mind and inner self know it is time to work magic. You may choose to do one or more of the following:

    🔥 Light a candle and/or incense
    🔥 Call upon the aid or presence of an entity to oversee what you are doing
    🔥 Ground and centre yourself
    🔥 Spend a few moments in quiet contemplation

2. Retrieve page 1 and your pencil/pen from wherever you stored them. Place them in front of you. Resist the urge to review your previous drawings. (I usually turn my paper face down, so I'm not tempted.)

3. While visualizing what perpetual prosperity looks like for you, say, "Powers of [planet of the day], infuse me with your wisdom and lead me deeper into understanding. Show me the way to perpetual prosperity."

4. Read the reflection on the planet of the day's contribution to perpetual prosperity and financial success, on page 126.

5. Spend some time meditating on these concepts and any others that come to mind. Allow yourself to be open to any thoughts that float into your head (if they don't seem to be related to the planet of the day, just allow them to float back out – but don't be too quick to dismiss them, because they could be there to give you important information).

6. Once you have finished meditating, it's time to sketch a doodle or design

in the planetary row of each column. Flip over your paper and get to work. In each column, refer to the row above and copy that design (or portions of it) into today's row. Let your intuition guide you as you make changes and additions to the previous design. Neither shape should be elaborate or overly detailed. If you get stuck on what to draw, throw some small sticks onto your table and gaze at the shapes they make. Allow yourself to casually sketch something in each column of the applicable row – one to represent the attributes of the planet you wish to embody (in the column under your name), and one to represent the planet's influence on perpetual prosperity (in the Personal Prosperity column).

7. Now here is the downright difficult part. The moment you are done sketching, put the paper away. Don't look at the images, don't review them, don't revise them. Just put the paper and pen away and extinguish the candle.

Day 9 – Saturday

This day is unlike all the others in this working. On this day, you won't do anything. There are no steps to perform today. It is Saturn's day and you have already worked with the power of this planet. Wait until tomorrow, the day of the Sun, to combine and refine the symbols you have created over the course of the week.

Day 10 – Sunday

GOAL – FINALIZATION OF YOUR PERSONAL PROSPERITY SIGIL

The goal of this day is:

- To combine the two separate sigils into your special, custom personal prosperity sigil.

Before we get started, congratulations are in order! You've made it to day 10 and are on the verge of completing a complex magical process. When you complete the steps below, you will have a powerful magical tool which you can use for a variety of purposes.

1. Begin by doing something to set the mood and let your subconscious mind and inner self know it is time to work magic. You may choose to do one or more of the following:
   - Light a candle and/or incense
   - Call upon the aid or presence of an entity to oversee what you are doing
   - Ground and centre yourself
   - Spend a few moments in quiet contemplation
2. Retrieve both page 1 and page 2 and your pencil/pen from wherever you stored them. Place page 1 in front of you.
3. By now, you should have completed two sigils. The one in the column labelled with your name represents you and all the different planetary influences you want to embody, as someone who is living the life of a perpetually prosperous person. The one in the column labelled Perpetual Prosperity represents all the external planetary influences you need to attain perpetual prosperity.
4. If you want to make any final changes to your sigils, now is the time to make them.
5. Once you are satisfied with the individual sigils, it is time to condense them into a single, final form. Use the second blank piece of paper you prepared back on day 1. Take your time.

Work to make the final sigil as simple and elegant as possible while still appealing to your magical senses. You will visualize and trace this shape often, so the simpler it is, the better.

6. When your intuition tells you your work is complete, make one final, clean copy of your new sigil. Put down your pen or pencil and admire your handiwork.

7. If you choose, you can ask for the final version to be blessed by the entity of your choice or some other magical power. For example, if you work with Domina Abundia (*see* Spiritual Allies, page 164), you could leave the sigil in front of an image of her overnight to ask for her blessing.

Full or Magickal Name		PERPETUAL PROSPERITY
♄ SATURN		
☉ SUN		
☽ MOON		
♂ MARS		
☿ MERCURY		
♃ JUPITER		
♀ VENUS		

PLANETARY MEDITATIONS/ REFLECTIONS

Saturn (ħ)

When Saturn comes to mind, it often brings thoughts of limitation and restriction. This planet's influence is often used in binding magic. How can it help achieve financial security and perpetual prosperity? Let's take a deeper look at the way the disciplinarian of the solar system can help you achieve your goals.

Saturn gets associated with limitation and restriction because it represents discipline, responsibility and patience. All these qualities are essential for achieving long-term goals like financial stability and endless prosperity.

With its serene rings and slow-but-steady pace through our solar system, Saturn reminds us that restraint and thoughtfulness are the bedrocks of serenity. Perpetual prosperity is an endless journey, which makes Saturn the perfect companion. Its steadying influence can help you establish healthy spending and money-management routines while banishing bad habits.

Saturn's air of authority can help you feel self-possessed, calm and confident as you explore topics that make you uncomfortable. Its power can help you gain the confidence to ask the right questions when making decisions about where and how to invest your time and money.

And of course, Saturn is always there to help you make the right choices when you are tempted to stray from your financial plan. This planet is on your side when you are fighting the forces of impulse spending or straying too far from your plans.

The Sun (☉)

The Sun is a fount of vitality and the endless source of energy that fuels our planet and everything on it. Its golden rays, reminiscent of the precious metal, are a reminder of the glorious abundance it bestows on all of us. It's no wonder that it has long represented wealth, financial security and fertility.

But the Sun represents something more. It is a symbol of ourselves, our lives and the paths we take through them. It lights our way, helping us to grow into the possibilities which are set before us.

The Sun's influence also blesses us with the feeling that everything will be alright. It lifts us out of gloom and worries, reassuring us that tomorrow is another day in which to face and conquer the challenges that lie in our paths. It can give us the boost of optimism we need to make one more attempt when all seems lost.

The Sun's unlimited power has often been associated with ideas about leadership, and while you may not command armies, you do have power over your own life and the choices you make. The Sun reminds you that you are ultimately in charge of your destiny and can make the changes you need to be a success.

All the energy of this celestial influence is ready to fuel your efforts to attain your goals.

The Moon (☽)

The moon, ever-changing, is a perfect symbol of an endless cycle of growth. Her tendency to augment intuition and psychic abilities can help you make important decisions about financial matters and next steps. But when we consider her influence on prosperity and wealth, we can't help but turn to her monthly journey through her phases. The lunar sphere is a celestial example that shows us the steps we must take, not once, but over and again, to achieve our goals.

The lunar cycle begins with the new moon, which can't be seen. The entire lunar surface is hidden. The dark of the moon is a contemplative time in which plans are made and intentions are set. It symbolizes the very beginning of a journey.

As the moon's crescent grows, it enters the waxing phase. As the illuminated portion of the moon's surface visibly grows in the night sky, it represents a time of expansion and development. This is the phase in which the hard work is done, and we begin to see the results of our labour.

When the moon is round and full in the sky, it represents a time that is reserved for recognizing and celebrating our accomplishments. This is the harvest, during which we can look back on what we have done during the waxing phase and assess our progress.

After the full moon passes, the lunar crescent begins to wane. This phase can represent a time of rest, but it also symbolizes an important opportunity to let go of the things that aren't helping us achieve our goals.

No matter what happens during a particular phase of the moon, it is important to remember that her cycle is endless. Her gentle influence can remind us that we must try more than once if we wish to succeed.

Mars (♂)

Mars carries with it associations of aggression and drive. Though Mars is usually considered the god of war, there are several ways that this planet's power can be used to fuel your financial ambitions and help you get things done.

This planet blazes red in the sky, even to the naked eye! The fiery energy of Mars's drive and aggression can be enough to get the most reluctant or timid person on their feet and motivated to persevere. If you are seeing red because you are tired of dealing with the same money problems time and time again, you can use Mars to inspire you to accomplish great deeds.

Acting as a catalyst, Mars can help spark things off and get things moving. It can help you apply the force you need to revitalize a stagnant situation or jolt yourself out of a rut. It can also give you the inspiration to initiate events and start new projects.

As Mars never hesitates to step onto the battlefield, this planet can give us the courage to make bold decisions and brave choices with our money. This planet also supports strategic thinking and making short-term plans that can help you achieve your goals.

Most importantly, Mars can provide the bravery we need to stand up for ourselves and make choices we know are in our best interests, even when we don't have support from others. This planet is an important ally in your fight for financial success.

Mercury (☿)

Mercury has the shortest orbit, hurtling around the Sun in only 88 days. Some people overlook this planet when it comes to prosperity magic, but when they do, it is to their detriment. Known for ruling communication, learning and research, Mercury is also the ruler of documents, negotiation and the marketplace.

This planet fans the flames of curiosity, prompting us to ask the "what if"s that help us dream big and set our sights on our highest goals. Its influence clarifies the mind when we are gathering and evaluating information and can help us figure out what we need to learn to make progress.

As Mercury is the planet of big ideas, it can feed prosperity by helping you come up with your next great idea or creative solution. It can also help facilitate communication, so you are able to articulate your needs and understand the needs of others. If you are dealing with contracts or paperwork of any kind, Mercury can help clear the way so you get what you need.

Under Mercury's influence, you will find it easier to negotiate and gain agreement from others, which comes in handy when you are buying or selling. With commerce and the marketplace firmly in its domain, Mercury can help your business flourish.

Mercury's influence can give you a silver tongue, so you are never at a loss for words. This blessing comes in handy when you are trying to make a deal or put your best foot forward while drafting résumés, filling out job applications, and answering questions during job interviews. If you need to pitch a project or ask for a raise, Mercury is firmly on your side, helping you find just the right words.

Jupiter (♃)

Jupiter is the planet of prosperity and wealth par excellence. Expansive and abundant, its influence can help you increase your wealth, identify opportunities and develop them. Under its power, all things grow and prosper. Jupiter's jovial influence is one of radiant and hopeful growth.

Jupiter's influence is illustrated by how all things grow, including our bank accounts. While the planet is a fount of abundance, it is also a reminder that things grow in fits and starts. There are times when it doesn't seem like much is happening, and there are times when the wealth and blessings roll in one after the other.

When focusing on Jupiter, it is important to remember its tendency to expand and elaborate on what is already present in your life. This planet can shower you with new ideas, endless abundance and perpetual growth. But its power can be overwhelming if it isn't approached in a balanced way. Tapping into its influences in conjunction with the other six planets helps to evenly disperse its abundant energy to all areas of your life. Consider Jupiter the abundance engine sitting at the heart of your magical work.

Allow Jupiter's powerful momentum to propel you to success by accepting the idea that opportunities for growth can appear anywhere. Even in the most hopeless situation, when you feel as though you are facing a dead end, Jupiter's endless bounty can turn things around at the last moment.

Venus (♀)

The planet most often associated with love and beauty, Venus can be a helpful ally in the quest for abundance and prosperity. As Venus is the goddess of love, she is an expert at using her subtle influence to help people attract what they desire. She is also a guide for building a beautiful and harmonious life.

THE GOLDEN GRIMOIRE

Venus's powers tend to attract the things we dwell upon, so we must be cautious about where our attention lies. It is also important to remember that Venus can see into our hearts and find our deepest desires. She can help you check in with yourself to determine if you really are pursuing the version of prosperity you most desire.

Under Venus's influence, we learn to appreciate beauty and harmony. The aesthetic side of wealth comes into play. The way your perfectly prosperous life manifests must be beautiful to you, or you are chasing someone else's dream.

As Venus encourages us to explore what we value, the planet serves as a reminder that there are many kinds of wealth and countless paths on which to seek it. Venus can help you find a path that is in harmony with your deepest desires and your sense of beauty.

As a final note, Venus rules Friday, which is traditionally payday in many parts of the world. So this planet can be seen as ruling over a day of financial culmination, when you get paid what you are due.

131

BUILDING A WEALTH ALTAR

A wealth altar will grow along with you and your financial needs. It will evolve over time to reflect your magical goals and ambitions as they develop and change. Not only will it give you a place to perform some of the spells in this book, but it will also infuse your household with the spirit of prosperity. It also offers a way to track your progress and gives you a concrete place to celebrate the many accomplishments that lie in your future.

When I explain how to create an altar, I usually start by telling people to figure out where they want to build their altar and then clear away any clutter. This method of building an altar starts with a cluttered space. (Either one that is already cluttered, or one that you make cluttered on purpose.) In the building of this altar, the clutter serves a purpose, because it represents all the baggage and outdated beliefs you have about money, finances and wealth. Clearing away the clutter in an intentional way can be one of the first steps you take to healing your wealth wounds and changing the way you think about prosperity.

THE GOLDEN GRIMOIRE

LOCATION

So let's talk about location and then discuss this all-important clutter. The best places to locate your wealth altar are:

- A place in your home where you do work for money or pay bills (an office or computer room)
- A place in your home where your family often gathers (a kitchen, dining room or living room)
- A place near the front door to welcome prosperity into your home
- The symbolic heart of your home (on a mantle or near a hearth)

You can also locate your altar in a place that is more private, like your bedroom or somewhere else in your house that isn't available to visitors. I like it when my wealth altar can store things like my magical diary and handbag/wallet. Whatever place you choose, it should be easily accessible and out of the way of foot traffic, so it doesn't get bumped or used as a convenient surface for keys, books and other stray items. (We want to start out cluttered, but we won't keep it that way!)

CLEARING CLUTTER

So about this clutter. Let's talk about it in detail. The flat surface you select might already be full of items, and that's a good starting point. But we don't want the clutter to represent just any old thing. We want it to symbolize any wealth wounds we may have. We want it to stand in for defeatist thoughts, misinformation and self-limiting beliefs. Take a look at what is on the surface of your future wealth altar, and see if you can relate any of it to your issues around money. Here are some examples:

- If there is a whole lot of anything (papers, pens, trash, knickknacks), it might represent debts, bills or any other financial worries.
- A chain or necklace could represent limitations or restrictions.

- A tool or kitchen utensil could represent money-making efforts from your past that didn't work.

Now, you may find that your chosen location doesn't have enough clutter. If you keep an exceptionally organized house, or your chosen surface just doesn't have the right kind of inspirational mess on it, fear not. You can still make use of this technique. You just need to intentionally clutter up the surface first. Here are some of the things you might add:

- Bills or slips of paper to represent debts or IOUs
- A small figurine of a house to represent rent or mortgage issues
- A wadded-up ball of aluminum foil to represent anxiety
- A tangled-up ball of string to represent confused emotions or difficult problems
- A small stack of coins to represent out-of-control spending

Spend some time considering what concepts you will link to your clutter because in this case, what you take off your altar is as important as what you will put on it. You may want to make a list of the items you want to start with on your altar and what they mean to you.

As with all personal altars, this one can be complex or simple. As long as your altar appeals to you and you feel comfortable working at it, then it doesn't matter what other people think of it. If it doesn't appeal to you and fill you with feelings of contentment, then it is working against you. So take the time to make sure you feel comfortable with everything you do.

As with many of the other spells and rituals in this book, clearing and rebuilding your altar may take several days. Don't rush things. Take your time and focus on each step.

PART 1: MAKING ROOM FOR WEALTH

TIMING

Do this part when the moon is waning.

SUPPLIES

- A cluttered space you intend to turn into a functioning wealth altar (naturally cluttered or one you prepared by cluttering it up beforehand)
- A list of what each item represents (if you have one)
- A tablecloth or large piece of paper if you prefer not to use cloth (select a colour that makes sense to you, such as green, silver or gold)
- A small bowl of water
- A clean cloth
- Salt
- Dried basil
- A white candle
- A candleholder
- Matches or a lighter

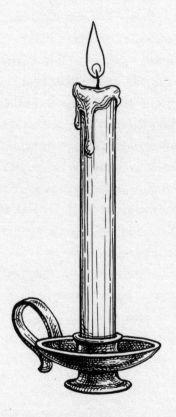

STEPS

1. Prepare yourself.
2. When you are ready, spread your hands over your future wealth altar and say, "This landscape is my prosperous wealth and any obstacles will now be cleared away."
3. Examine the items on your future altar space. For each item:
   - Wait until an item catches your eye or interests you.
   - Pick up the item.
   - Hold it and give it a close look.
   - Think about how it represents some aspect of yourself or your beliefs about your potential for wealth you want to eliminate.
   - When you are ready, say something like, "This [item] represents [aspect]. As I remove it from my sacred space of wealth, so I remove it from myself."
     Example: "This pile of papers represents my debts. As I remove it from my sacred space of wealth, so I remove them from myself." Or: "This necklace represents my feelings of limitation and inhibition when it comes to wealth. As I remove it from my sacred space, so I remove it from myself."
   - Take the item and put it somewhere else, far from your future altar (preferably where it belongs). If something needs to be thrown out, put it in the trash. If a necklace needs to be put away, put it in your jewellery box. As you do, remind yourself that each concept or self-image has its place, and you have the power to put it where it belongs.
4. When all the items have been removed and put away, take a few moments to enjoy the clear, calm space you have made.
5. Make some blessing water.
   - Put some water in a bowl.
   - Put three pinches of salt in the water and say, "Creature of earth, cleanse this water so that it may do my bidding."

- Put three pinches of basil in the water and say, "Blessed plant, infuse this water with your essence so that you may drive away all disruptive influences from everything it touches."

6. Dip a cloth in the water, wring it out well and wipe down the surface of your altar. If possible, wipe down its legs or other surfaces. Visualize the blessed water infusing the area with a clear white light that drives away all disruptive influences.

7. When the surface of the altar is dry, put a tablecloth or coloured piece of paper on your altar.

8. Put a white candle in a holder. Put the holder in the centre of your altar and light it. Say, "Bring light and blessings to this space and prepare it for my work."

Wait until the moon is waxing before completing part 2. While you wait, be sure to keep the space clear. You can also occasionally burn white candles in the space until you can finish building your altar. I strongly recommend journalling at this time, paying particular attention to the results of the clearing ritual. You will likely experience significant dreams or receive other messages. Spend at least one journalling session crafting your statement of intent for your altar, which you will use in the next part.

PART 2: BUILDING YOUR ALTAR

As the first step on the road to wealth is clearing away old ideas about money and finances that no longer serve you, keep this altar simple and uncluttered. The altar will grow and change with you over time, reflecting the magical work you do.

If you have been waiting for the waxing moon to build this altar, hopefully you have been able to keep the space you cleared empty and clean. However, don't despair if you haven't! If you feel like you need to reinforce the clarity of the space, remake the blessing water from part 1 and ritually wipe down your altar space. If you have already placed a green tablecloth, you can flick it with some blessing water to cleanse it before proceeding. These steps aren't necessary, but I want to mention them in case you feel like you didn't maintain your previous work.

If you are planning to work with a specific entity, this is an opportunity to start building a relationship with them if you haven't already. *See* page 164 for information about various entities you might want to explore working with.

If you have created a personal prosperity sigil, you can incorporate it into your altar as a secret hidden element that only you and the other people using the altar know about.

TIMING
Do this part when the moon is waxing.

SUPPLIES

- Two matching candleholders
- Two green candles
- A shallow bowl
- An image of an entity you want to work with (optional)
- A supply of frankincense or cinnamon incense
- An incense holder
- A square of gold or yellow paper (optional)
- A green marker (optional)

STEPS

1. If you want to incorporate your personal prosperity sigil:
   - If you have a cloth on your altar space, remove it.
   - Use a green marker or pen to draw your sigil on yellow paper.
   - Place the sigil face up in the centre of your altar space.
2. If you need to do so, replace your altar covering (either the cloth or paper).
3. Announce the purpose of your altar. This is a highly personalized statement of intention that you should plan carefully. It may be something like, "I build this altar to clear the way between me and perpetual wealth." Make the statement something specific and concrete.
4. Arrange the following items on your altar space:
   - If you are working with an entity, place an image of them at the back centre of the space.
   - Place the candles in their candleholders at the back corners of the space.
   - Place the shallow bowl in the centre of the space.
   - Place the incense in front of the bowl.
5. Light the candles and incense.
6. Spend time meditating on the purpose of your wealth altar. If you are working with an entity, speak with them and explain your intent for the altar and the help you need to achieve it.

FOUNDATIONS OF FINANCIAL MAGIC

USING YOUR WEALTH ALTAR

Now that you have cleared a space for it and built a beautiful altar, let's spend some time thinking about ways you can incorporate it into your magical work.

- The shallow bowl in the centre of your altar is a representation of your ability to collect and hold wealth. Some folks choose to put their pocket change in the bowl to symbolize growing wealth. Others store their wallet in the bowl to bless it and keep it full. Use the bowl as a place to leave gifts if you are working with any spiritual entities on your journey to wealth.
- If your altar is big enough, you can do your magical work on it. Otherwise, you can put the results of your magical work on your altar. For example, you could prepare a money-drawing candle at your kitchen table but burn it on your wealth altar once it is ready.
- Store your magical money-making tools (like the Money-Drawing Shaker Box on page 200) on or near your altar so you always know where to find them.
- If you decide to stop carrying your credit or debit card, bury it under the pocket change or bills you have placed in the bowl in the centre of your altar. Ask that the entity you are working with strengthen your willpower when it comes to spending.

HEALING WEALTH WOUNDS
USING YOUR WEALTH ALTAR

As mentioned before, it takes repetition and patience to fully heal yourself from all the wealth wounds you are carrying. Your wealth altar can help you reduce the power of your wealth wounds and clear them from your mind.

1. Cut out some small slips of paper and store them in the shallow bowl in the centre of your altar.
2. Keep a red pen near or on your altar.
3. When you find yourself thinking something negative about your earning potential, right to be financially comfortable or ability to achieve your goals, make a note of it.
4. As soon as you can, go to your altar, remove a slip of paper from the bowl, and write the thought on it using the red pen.
5. Put the thought back in the bowl. Ask that it be banished from your way of thinking now and in the future.
6. Let the thought sit in the bowl for 12–24 hours.
7. Take the slip of paper with the thought out of the bowl.
8. Dispose of it. (I usually burn it over my sink. However, this can be dangerous, so please use caution and do what is right for you.)

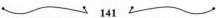

MAINTAINING YOUR WEALTH ALTAR

One of the main purposes of a wealth altar is to infuse your household and surroundings with positive influences which will draw prosperity and wealth to you. Just like all altars, it requires regular maintenance so it can work well.

- Most importantly, spend time at your altar sitting and listening to whatever messages you may receive. An altar is a space where the physical and the spiritual can meet. The more you use it, the more likely it is that you will receive guidance and assistance there when you need it most.

- Dust your altar. Remove all the items from it and gently dust the surface with a clean cloth. Dust each item before putting it back.

- If you choose to leave offerings of food or drink on your altar, make sure to remove them within three days.

- Decorate or rearrange the items on your altar as your intuition prompts you to. You might find the perfect rock or a beautiful leaf, and feel moved to put it on your altar. If so – do it!

- Pick a cadence for maintaining your altar. Remember that more doesn't necessarily mean better. Pick a frequency that works for you and your schedule. It's better to work with your altar consistently once a month than to feel guilt or pressure because you decide to do it daily but regularly miss days. Here are three options you might choose:

1. Once a month on the full moon
2. Weekly, every Friday
3. Daily, before bedtime

A WEALTH OF MAGICAL CORRESPONDENCES

The Colours of Wealth

Choosing colours that correspond to your intention is a simple way to increase the power and impact of your magical work. Whether you are picking out an altar cloth, choosing a crystal or selecting a candle to burn, using a meaningful colour that complements your intent can help ensure your success. Colours are powerful tools not only because they carry magical correspondences but also because they can strongly influence your mood and attitude.

I live in the US where, regardless of denomination, all paper money is the same green colour. So whenever I think about cash, finances or wealth, that colour immediately comes to mind. Green works well symbolically because it also represents things like growth and newness, which are wonderful concepts to include in wealth magic. If you live or work outside the US, I encourage you to take the colour of your local currency into account. In spells in this book that call for using green to represent money, consider using a colour that makes more sense to you locally. For example, when I lived in Australia, where yellow is the predominant colour on the $50 note, I would often use that colour to represent money when I worked spells for fast cash. Yellow was great because it reminded me of the Sun and gold, both of which are related to ideas of wealth and financial success.

There are many different systems of colour correspondence out there for you to try. However, just like the card interpretations in "Tarot: A Helpful Tool During Your Financial Journey", I want to provide you with a list of colour correspondences that are focused on wealth magic and financial matters. You will also find examples of when and how to use these colours, but the options are limitless. Use your creativity to come up with your own techniques.

How to use colour magic

Colours have a powerful influence on both our psyches and our magical workings. They carry powerful correspondences that are so easy to put to use! Here are a few simple ways you can put the power of colour magic to work for you:

- Get dressed! To incorporate the power of a colour into your daily adventures, wear something of that colour. For an extra boost, make sure the colour is visible to others. But wearing the colour as an undergarment can provide you with a secret source of magical power.
- Visualization! It only takes a second to close your eyes and picture a colour so you can focus on and internalize the correspondence related to it. If you have the time, picture the colour surrounding you in a bright glow.
- Choose your tools! Customize your spells by choosing candles, paper or other magical components of a colour that corresponds to your specific needs.
- Dress up your wealth altar! If you have set up or are building a wealth altar and have a specific long-term goal, choose altar decorations of a colour that matches your intent.

The colours

Black – A shield of strength and protection, black can help you ward off negative or disruptive energies. Black transmits feelings of authority and solemnity, so it is a great colour to wear when you want to appear polished, professional and in control. Burn black candles to help banish obstacles that stand in the way of achieving your financial goals. Carry a black crystal to protect yourself from bad spending habits.

Brown – Earthy and stabilizing, brown is a colour that can be turned to when you want to ensure things remain just as they are. This grounding colour helps to slow things down and keep things steady. If you are worried about upcoming changes that might put a strain on your finances, burn a brown candle to slow them down so that you have more time to prepare. Carry a brown stone to help remain grounded in the midst of change. If you have a goal that requires slow and constant change, brown is the colour to turn to.

Crimson – A colour made of a blend of red and yellow (*see* their individual correspondences below), crimson combines the best of both hues. This colour symbolizes a blend of passion and vitality and can be used to strengthen and energize your financial plans. Burn a crimson candle during the course of any project or task to give it an extra boost of energy. Carry three or five coins of the same denomination in a small crimson bag to draw money to your pocket.

Gold – Radiant and luminous, gold is a beacon of wealth and prosperity. Gold is associated with the Sun and vibrancy. Use it when you are working on long-term or complex financial goals. Dress your altar or sacred space with gold-coloured decorations to align your household with your long-term financial goals. Wear something gold (jewellery or the colour) when you want to project financial competence and responsibility.

Green – A symbol of perennial and constant growth, green is a colour of flourishing development. It represents the harvest that comes after hard work. The colour of currency in the US, it is used frequently in all manner of prosperity and wealth spells. Spend some time relaxing and meditating in green spaces to focus your mind and establish a prosperous mindset. Carry a green stone like aventurine in your pocket or purse to attract abundance.

Grey – A colour not commonly used in magic, grey can help you overcome obstacles and persist in the face of difficulties. You can use the light of a grey candle to help you navigate difficult situations, particularly if you need to figure out the right thing to say. If you have a spell in process and it seems to be in trouble, you can burn a grey candle to support or augment your ongoing work. Carry a grey stone like labradorite to ensure your plans go smoothly.

Light blue – Calming and tranquil, light blue can help evoke clarity and peace of mind. If you are feeling nervous or as though you can't focus, wear something light blue to boost your morale and help you collect your thoughts. Burn a blue candle when you are formulating your plans or wear a ring with a blue stone to keep your mind on track.

Orange – A little dash of orange can give you a burst of energy and clear your mind. Its influence will help you clear away mental and physical clutter. If you have been avoiding a task, put on an orange shirt or tie your hair up in an orange scarf, light an orange candle, and get to work! The colour helps boost your courage and stimulate your creativity.

Pink – A colour that isn't just reserved for love spells. Pink symbolizes success and accomplishment. It also symbolizes clean living, so you can use it when you are trying to eliminate a bad habit or rein in your spending. A small bunch of pink flowers or a pink cloth on your altar can help boost your positivity and self-image.

Purple – When you want to command attention and make your voice heard, purple is a staunch ally. It is a colour of regal ambition and self-mastery and historically was reserved for royalty. Wear purple when you are pursuing your ambitions or trying to maintain control of a situation. Use purple ink when journalling about your grandest goals. Burning purple candles can help you overcome business or career obstacles.

Red – Symbolizing fiery passion and power, red can ignite your ambitions and drive. Red can be used as the symbolic fuel for all your financial plans. It also symbolizes health and vitality, so it is an excellent choice when you are working to protect and strengthen your health. Carrying a red stone, like garnet, can help you gain the energy and strength of mind to accomplish your goals.

Silver – Luxurious yet mysterious, silver is another colour that is traditionally associated with money. It symbolizes hard work paying off and the slow, steady building of a nest egg. Burning silver candles can help you achieve financial stability. A silver altar cloth can enhance your psychism and help you intuitively and creatively craft your financial plans.

White – Clear and cleansing, white is a colour of spiritual strength and purification. When doing magical or spiritual work, you can use it to replace any other colour because it can represent anything. Burn a white candle to heal yourself from spiritual wounds and reinforce your intentions. Use white flowers in your office or in your sacred space to keep your spirits up.

Yellow – Bright and cheerful, yellow attracts abundance and opportunities. It can be used in place of gold, if necessary. This colour can draw things to you, so carrying a yellow stone like citrine can attract money. When doing sigil magic, a yellow highlighter can be used to turn any piece of paper into a luxurious golden backdrop for money-drawing and prosperity sigils.

Your favourite colour – Whatever your favourite colour is, it is important to your magical work. Don't underestimate the effect that wearing your favourite outfit can have on your confidence and sense of wellbeing. Many people strongly identify with their favourite colour, so you can use a candle of that colour to represent yourself in your magical work. For example, I love orange, so I can take an orange candle, carve my name and date of birth into it (or astrological information) and create a tool that I can work on to effect change upon myself. If you are doing work for other people, you can ask them what their favourite colour is so you can use it to represent them.

Combining colours

One powerful way to incorporate colour into your magical work is to identify two or more colours that will help you accomplish your specific goals. *See the Banishing Paperwork Panic candle spell on page 250 as a demonstration of how combining colours can add to your magical repertoire.*

TREASURE FROM THE EARTH

By their very nature, crystals and stones are wealth symbols because they remind us of treasure. Choosing a beautiful crystal to use as the focal point of your magic or a favourite piece of jewellery to incorporate into a spell adds beauty and a feeling of luxury and abundance to your work. It's important to remember that you don't need a perfect specimen of a stone for it to bestow the influences you need. The piece just needs to speak to you.

How to use gemstone magic

Glimmering and beguiling, gemstones are a major component of a lot of magical workings. There are many simple ways to include them in your practices. Try out these techniques the next time you'd like a magical financial boost.

- Bedazzle yourself! There's nothing like wearing a favourite piece of magical jewellery to increase your confidence and provide a magical boost to your day. Wearing a piece in any location can give you the help you need, but you can target a gemstone's influence by wearing it in a specific place on your body:
  - Earrings, to filter what you hear and provide you with the ability to fully understand the meaning behind it
  - Anklets, to help guide your steps and lead you in the right direction or protect you from going the wrong way
  - Short necklaces and chokers, to influence your speech and communication
  - Longer necklaces over your heart, to protect your heart or strengthen it
  - Bracelets, to guide your hands when working or making things
  - Rings, to guide your hands when working or making things. Each finger is related to a different planetary influence, so you can fine-tune the influence the gemstone will have on you or enhance its powers:
    - **Thumb: Mars** – conflict and resolution, confidence, initiation of ideas or plans
    - **First finger: Jupiter** – expansion, growth, generosity, development, celebration
    - **Middle finger: Saturn** – restriction, limitation, control, discipline
    - **Ring finger: Sun** – Enjoyment, creativity, partnership
    - **Pinky: Mercury** – Communication, commerce, exchange
- Take a rest! Sleeping with a gemstone can help you absorb

its influence. You can keep one on your bedside table, under your pillow or in your pillowcase, or for long-term influence, you can tuck it between your mattress and boxspring. Depending on the size and nature of the gem, you may wish to put it in a gauze or flannel bag first.

- Take time out for meditation! Enter a state of relaxation while holding a crystal in your hand. Explore the energy of the stone to discover how you can work with it to achieve your goals.

- Decorate your home or workspace! Tucking a crystal into a key location can help you maintain an aura or atmosphere of prosperity and focus. Even if the crystal is out of sight in a desk drawer, its influence will still be felt. Or if you can, put it out on display to beautify your space and remind you it is working.

- Decorate your altar! Crystals and gemstones are a fantastic addition to your wealth altar. You may even wish to store your more magically significant pieces of jewellery in or on your altar so they can contribute their influences to your work.

THE GOLDEN GRIMOIRE

The crystals

Amazonite – This stone's colours range from a refreshing green to a soothing blue-green. It is a powerful ally for people seeking luck and working on developing financial prospects. It encourages calculated risk-taking, making it a favourite for entrepreneurs and investors. This stone will bring you opportunities to take careful and calculated risks. If you are ready to make big and bold changes, this stone could be for you.

Amber – Despite not being an actual stone, the fossilized resin that makes up amber carries potent energy for attracting prosperity and opportunities. It also helps promote creativity, not just artistically but also when it comes to problem-solving and planning. It is invaluable for small-business owners and creatives alike. Amber's warm energy helps to keep projects vital and active. It can also free up stagnant energy, supporting long-term efforts to accomplish a goal.

Amethyst – A regal stone with a long history, amethyst's purple hue has been associated with royalty for centuries. It evokes an atmosphere of wealth and largess. Amethyst offers protection from financial misfortunes, and ensures that justice prevails. If you have to deal with legal proceedings of any type, amethyst will help ensure justice runs its course and proper procedures are followed.

Aventurine – A versatile stone that ranges in colour from pale to dark green, aventurine is prized for its ability to attract wealth and success. Its gentle energy aids in emotional healing, so it can provide a supportive aura for working through financial worries and recovering from debt. This stone can help you disengage from the past so you can focus on the future.

Black tourmaline – Famous as a stone used for protection, black tourmaline shields against disruptive influences that might impede progress in your career or toward your financial goals. It is grounding and helps to banish anxiety. If you have it on hand, it will help you focus and think clearly even when under pressure. Carry it when you don't want your worries to get the best of you.

Citrine – A stone long associated with the Sun, citrine looks like a drop of sunshine. Its beautiful yellow colour helps elevate your mood. However, for money magic, we should be more interested in its ability to amplify your efforts to build and consolidate wealth. This stone helps you address your future with joy and positivity. It also increases psychic abilities, providing the opportunity for intuitive solutions to any money concerns you might have.

Emerald – A luxurious stone associated with wealth and living the high life, emerald may seem like an expensive choice. But even a rough uncut emerald can help draw abundance. This stone is perfect for someone in sales, as it leads you to new prospects and business opportunities. It's a magnet for positive attention so it can help you advertise your business, highlight your efforts and show off your accomplishments in the best light.

Fire opal – Are you chasing your dreams and trying to transmute them into a career? If so, fire opal will help you combine your passions and ambitions. Its fiery energy inspires action and creativity and will propel you toward success in your career. Whether you are starting out on a new adventure or seeking to overcome obstacles, this stone can evoke confidence and motivation, reinforcing your dedication and drive.

Garnet – This dark red stone is a catalyst for growth. It empowers people to escape stagnant or repetitive situations to pursue a new way of life. Whether you want to break free from bad habits or chart a new course of action, garnet can support you with strength and resolve so you can accomplish your goals.

Green calcite – A stone of prosperity and renewal, green calcite will infuse your financial efforts with fresh energy and vitality. It helps to promote expansion while protecting what you have already accomplished, barring disruptive influences from your presence. If things feel chaotic and hectic, green calcite can help smooth things out with its gentle power.

Iolite – A beautifully violet-coloured stone, iolite is often praised for its ability to develop your psychic abilities. However, it also helps with the elimination of debts and the breaking of established patterns, making it a great stone for reducing destructive spending habits. This gem often contains traces of iron, so think of it as giving you an iron resolve when it comes to sticking to your budget.

Jade – Though green is probably the first colour that springs to mind when you think about jade, it comes in a variety of colours, including shades of blue, lavender and gold. It is a stone of luxury and wealth and can help usher these things into your life. However, its most interesting attribute is the ability to help you build a positive and accepting mindset when it comes to wealth. It's a great stone to carry when you are working on healing wealth wounds.

Malachite – Polished malachite often displays stunning bands of colour that range from light to dark green all the way through to black. Copper helps give this stone its green hue, so it is used for healing spiritual illnesses and can help you recover from wealth wounds. It is also a powerful stone for attracting business success and putting things to rights after a mistake has been made.

Moss agate – A visually stunning stone that looks like threads of moss embedded in a clear or milky background, moss agate is famed for strengthening your connection to nature and helping plants and gardens grow. The presence of moss agate can help ensure high yields and an abundant harvest. Therefore, it is also associated with wealth that is gathered over time. Its connection with nature also makes it a stone beloved by treasure hunters, because it can help uncover things of value.

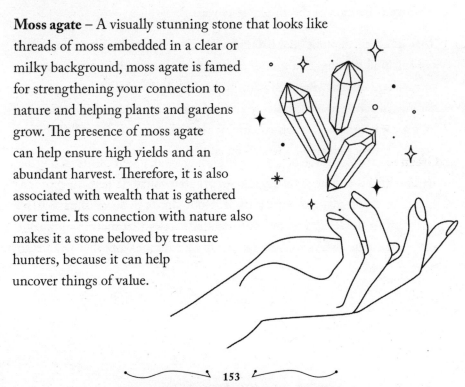

FOUNDATIONS OF FINANCIAL MAGIC

Peridot – These stones are a gorgeous golden-green and they can both help you achieve your financial goals and protect you from any jealousy that may spring up due to your financial accomplishments. In addition to these attributes, peridot helps support a healthy and prosperous business and can draw money to your enterprises.

Pyrite – Also called fool's gold, this beautiful stone glows with the colour and sheen of gold but is much more affordable. Even though it's not the real thing, it still generates an aura of luck that brings prosperity and abundance your way. It also helps you speak your truth, so it can come in handy when you need to speak up for yourself and your plans.

Red coral – Another entry in this list that isn't really a stone or mineral, red coral is the skeleton of a marine animal that was originally primarily found in the Mediterranean Sea. In addition to protecting you from envy, coral can help you correct your financial problems. It is also the perfect stone to carry or wear to job interviews or when you are asking for a promotion. When shopping for red coral, look for unworked branches rather than pieces that have been carved into beads or other shapes. It is believed that unworked "living" coral is the most powerful.

Rose quartz – A stone that is famous for its ability to facilitate emotional and spiritual healing, rose quartz can be helpful in nearly any scenario. It is an excellent choice when you want to heal past spiritual wounds, promote feelings of self-love and forgive yourself for past mistakes. Rose quartz can be a great companion when you are working through financial truths and exploring your personal beliefs about wealth.

Ruby – This is a stone of luxury and wealth, but you don't need an expensive specimen to do magical work with it. Ruby draws in success, particularly related to your career and business dealings. It can help attract money to you, particularly when you are waiting to be paid for work that has already been completed.

Salt – Though it is a common substance today, salt used to be so highly prized that it was used to pay Roman soldiers (which is where we get the word "salary"). As well as being an excellent tool for spiritual cleansing, it can support magical workings for stability and steady work. It is a symbol of a safe home and consistent income.

Sapphire/Yellow sapphire – Another one of those luxury stones often found in high-end jewellery, sapphire brings opulent wealth to mind – but that's not why it is on this list. The blue variety, which is the most common, helps to dispel fraud and lies as well as assisting in obtaining justice when you are involved in legal proceedings. Meanwhile, the yellow variety helps inspire you and get you moving when you are faced with a challenge.

Selenite – An inexpensive stone closely associated with lunar energies, selenite also surrounds you with lucky vibes, so it can help you when you feel down or like the Fates are working against you. It is also known for spiritual healing, so it can help you recover from wealth wounds or anxiety.

Sunstone – There is natural sunstone, which is a type of feldspar that can have a translucent orange colour. There is also synthetic sunstone, which is opaque and comes in a variety of colours. Synthetic sunstone looks like it has been infused with glitter. You can use either variety to attract prosperity and draw money. Either variety can also protect your financial situation from unexpected debts and other catastrophes.

Tiger's eye – A stone that displays brown and golden bands when it is polished, tiger's eye can help balance your emotions. It is included in this list because it can also help open your eyes so you can see things as they really are. It can strengthen your resolve and help you stick to a plan. This stone can also reenergize you when you are in the middle of a process or cycle so you can see it through to the end.

A GARDEN OF ABUNDANCE

When working with concepts of growth and abundance, the sustaining and supporting nature of herbs and plants contributes significantly to magical workings. If you have a green thumb, using plants you've grown on your own is particularly powerful. But you can also use dried and fresh plants you purchase with great success. Below is a short list of herbal correspondences specific to prosperity and wealth magic.

How to use herbal magic

Herbs are easy to find, and you can use them as living plants or as dried powders and roots. It is important to note that you should take a careful approach when working with them, especially if you are using a herb you haven't interacted with before. There's no way to tell if you will have an allergic reaction to something, so before you bathe in or consume a herb, test it out carefully. Here are some ways to incorporate herbs into your magical life:

- Have a relaxing cuppa! The easiest and safest way to do this is to find a pre-made commercial mix that contains herbs with the influences you wish to imbibe. Or you can make your own herbal blending, using herbs you know you can consume safely. Drinking a relaxing tea can help prepare you for magical work or any important event.

- Go take a soak! Make up a herbal sachet and use it to infuse the water of your bath. This works great for cleansing yourself or blessing yourself with the herbs' influences.

- Whip up a meal! Whether you want to make a simple snack or a hearty meal, herbs can be an important magical addition. You could plan an entire meal where all the dishes contribute to your goals, or you might just want to sprinkle some cinnamon on your toast while you work on your gratitude journal.

- Carry some with you! A small flannel bag with a blend of herbs that support your goals is an inconspicuous way to bring the influence of your herbs with you. Toss the bag in your handbag or pocket. Or you could even put a small sprinkle of herbs in your wallet.

- Get growing! If you have a green thumb or just want to experiment with growing your own herbs, give it a shot. Herbs can be grown inside or outside, as long as they can get enough sun. You can keep your fresh plants in significant places in your home and incorporate caring for them into your daily magical routines.

- Spice up your altar! A sprinkle of herbs on your wealth altar or in your blessing bowl can help support your magical goals and contribute more energy to your magical work.

The herbs

> **Note:**
> While toxic herbs are marked in this list, please realize that you should not eat any herb without knowing if you are allergic to it.

Alfalfa – A powerful ward against poverty and lack, this herb can help build a buffer between you and financial difficulties. If you are in dire need and are concerned about putting food on your table, it can bless you and help keep your head above water. It can also help banish feelings of desperation and need, clearing the way for doing successful magical work, so consider it a medicine for healing wealth wounds.

Allspice – For a long time, I thought allspice was a herbal mixture due to its name. But it is actually a single herb. It is also a strong catalyst that adds power to spells and helps contribute strength when you incorporate it into a magical working, amplifying your efforts.

Basil – While well known for attracting positive energy and banishing disruptive influences, this cosy herb has additional useful attributes that can contribute to your journey toward wealth. It has a calming influence and can help centre your mind when you are under stress. It also contributes to building a sound and happy career, so turn to it if you are trying to develop your career path or seek a new job.

Bay leaf – A powerful manifestation herb, bay is famous for bringing you what you seek. Write what you want to achieve on a whole bay leaf and incorporate it into spells for manifestation. Bay also drives away disruptive influences that can obstruct your progress, so burning the herb or putting whole leaves on your windowsill can keep your household happy and prosperous.

Bayberry [TOXIC] – This herb is famous for attracting money. As the saying goes, "A bayberry candle burned to the socket brings joy to your life and money to your pocket." In addition to bringing money into your life, it can also help you curtail your spending and build your savings. Buy and burn bayberry candles to assist you in your efforts to consolidate your cash.

Bergamot – This lovely citrus fruit appears in Earl Grey tea due to its calming influence. It soothes the mind when it is troubled. It also grounds excess energy so you can relax physically as well as mentally. When it comes to financial magic, bergamot can draw luck to and bless your career. As it is calming, it's a great scent to work with when you are asking for a raise or headed to a job interview.

Camomile – These beautiful flowers are little rays of sunshine and are closely associated with the Sun, so they are closely tied to prosperity and growth. Like bergamot above, they are famous for their relaxing influence. They also draw abundance and opportunities as well as bringing you a touch of luck.

Cinnamon – This herb is famously used in a monthly spell to welcome wealth into the home (blowing a pinch of cinnamon through the front door into your house on the first of each month), so its ability to draw money and prosperity is well known. However, it also helps maintain awareness of everything you already have and brings about feelings of warmth and gratitude.

Cinquefoil – Also known as five-finger grass, this herb blesses any and all work the five fingers can do. It is an excellent assistant for people who sell handcrafted items or for anyone who wants to highlight their skills.

Clove – Powerfully protective, this herb will build a wall between you and any negativity or disruption that is thrown your way. It makes space for luck, allowing the room for good things to come to you.

Irish moss – This is the perfect herb for enhancing and developing your business prospects. It will help protect your business interests and draw in sales. It will also aid you in making a good impression with clients and customers.

Jasmine – I will admit that when I think of this herb, my first thoughts aren't about money! For me, jasmine brings to mind ideas of romance and passion. However, these decadent flowers also draw money and enhance your intuition. If you want to delve into your subconscious to identify wealth wounds or to understand a financial situation more deeply, this is the herb to use.

Lemongrass – The aura from this herb is bright and light. It can help elevate your energy and personality when you are going to a job interview, as well as shed light on difficulties when you are trying to figure out what to do next. It lightens the heart and brings an optimistic viewpoint. It is an excellent companion when you are problem-solving or planning.

Marigold – These beautiful flowers look like little solar discs, so they instantly call to mind prosperity. They are a symbol of constancy and can help you stick to your financial plans. Not only do they draw good fortune, but they are famed for attracting the souls of the dead, so you can use them for ancestral work.

Mint – I love this herb because it is easy to grow (but it will take over your whole backyard if you aren't careful)! It is also an excellent dual-action herb because it clears away disruptive influences and attracts money. Easy to find and work with, mint can be used when you are wanting to clear away obstacles between you and financial success.

Nutmeg – This herb is famous for drawing wealth and luck. You can use powdered nutmeg in spells or carry a whole nutmeg in your purse or pocket to draw prosperity. Warming and cosy, this herb can contribute its powers to happy home spells and be used to make your workplace feel more inviting.

Oregano – This herb can cleanse away difficulties and help you obtain a new perspective on your life. It brings cheer and happiness into the home, but it also draws cash to your wallet. Oregano can help draw you out of the depths of depression while developing a willingness to meet your challenges head-on.

Patchouli – An earthy, grounding herb that helps eliminate excess energy, patchouli can help you keep your bearings when it seems like everything around you is in transition. It also helps banish disruptive influences at the same time. On top of that, working with patchouli can help manifest your desires, so it is perfect for prosperity and wealth magic.

Rosemary – A herb often associated with capturing memories or enhancing recall, rosemary is also quite helpful for prosperity magic. I work with it when the energy around me feels sluggish or I feel down on my luck. If you need an energetic reset to get back on track, rosemary attracts positive energy and generates good luck.

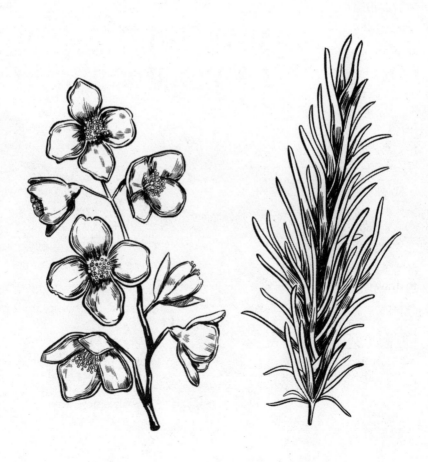

THE GOLDEN GRIMOIRE

HOW TO USE
THIS SECTION

The grimoire starts with a short exploration of some of the spiritual allies that can support your journey to abundance. If you don't already work with a spiritual ally for wealth magic, you can take some inspiration from the entities listed here.

The spells in this grimoire have been broken up into three general categories: Money, Prosperity and Wealth, but they don't have to be worked in order.

🔥 Spells in the Money section focus on quickly attracting small sums of cash, protecting your property, and turning your luck from bad to good.

🔥 Spells in the Prosperity section focus on getting and keeping a job, maintaining or improving your position at work, and supporting the earners in your household.

🔥 Spells in the Wealth section focus on handling more complex financial situations, generating money on your own terms (like running your own business), and gratitude.

The section on Group Work gives you ideas for adapting individual spells into group workings as well as general guidelines for designing your own group rituals.

Please note that because I wanted to fit as many spells and charms as possible into this book, none of them include steps for preparing yourself, preparing your workspace or wrapping up the spell by disposing of the remnants of your work. You can find that information in the Appendix on page 298.

SPIRITUAL ALLIES

This section is a short overview of spiritual entities you might want to experiment working with on your magical journey to wealth. Please note that this is just a small sampling of the numerous beings you could choose to ally with. As with all things magical, you may immediately feel a strong calling to work with a particular being, or it might take time and experimentation to find the one that wants to partner with you. Either path is an equally moving journey of discovery, so take it slow and enjoy building relationships with the being(s) you choose (or who choose you).

To be as inclusive as possible, I've tried to select entities from various belief systems from around the world. Some I have worked with, and some my friends have worked with. As always, if you feel moved to interact and work with an entity from outside your culture, be respectful. Make the effort to approach the entity in a way that appreciates and acknowledges the originating culture. Be sure to work with the entity within its proper context. Approach the entity with deep respect and if you get the message that it doesn't want to work with you, don't press the issue. There are plenty of spiritual allies out there who are ready to help you.

Use this list to generate ideas as a starting point for further explorations. Engaging with a new entity takes work and dedication.

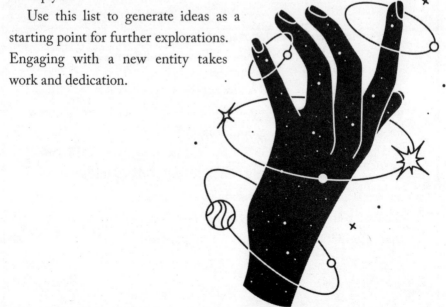

GETTING STARTED

The best way to work with any spiritual entity is to build a long-term relationship with them. In order to do so, you need to understand not only their attributes but how they function in the context of the culture and society they come from. That means the first step to building a relationship consists of a lot of research. You can find information in books and online, but you must ensure that you are working from accurate sources. The best way to gather information is to talk to people who are part of the culture and can help you fully understand the entity. That might sound like a frustratingly large amount of effort – but consider it as a way to build a bridge to that entity so that you can approach them respectfully.

Once your research is complete, include an image of the entity on your altar or in a special place in your home. At this stage, make simple offerings to the entity. Spend time each day communicating with the entity via meditation or prayer. Make sure you use some of that time to listen for any responses or information from the entity.

At any point in this process, you may feel as though working with this entity isn't right. The feeling may emanate from yourself or from the entity. If this happens, don't try to force the issue. You are meant to work with someone else, so it is time to seek that other entity out.

Once you feel the time is right, and as though a healthy relationship has been established, you can incorporate the entity into your magical and spiritual work. Here are some of the ways you can do that:

- Write them petitions asking for help
- Pray to them for help and support
- Ask them to contribute power to your magical work
- Ask them to bless your spiritual or magical efforts

POTENTIAL ENTITIES

Abundantia/Domina Abundia

Abundantia's name is a big hint that she is the Roman goddess of abundance and prosperity. She is also called Copia (think of the word "copious", meaning abundant). She rules all features of wealth, including savings, investments, cash flow and important purchases. A benevolent goddess, she ensures that there are always plenty of resources to care for your family and meet your goals. She is a protector of valuables and a defender of prosperity.

Though there aren't a lot of stories about her in the folkloric record, she appears in art and on Roman coins, often pouring out a cornucopia of wealth and treasures.

Abundantia may be related to the folklore figure Domina Abundia (Mistress Abundance). Her behaviour aligns with Italian *Fate* (fairy) beliefs. She is also related to the cornucopia and to agricultural tools. Homeowners leave out food and drink offerings for her overnight. If she approves of the offerings, she blesses the home with prosperity and wealth.

Offerings:

Water, wine, olives, olive oil, bread, sweets

Work with her when:

You are seeking abundance and a serene, comfortable household.

Ancestors

Ancestors, particularly those who were good at building wealth or running households, are excellent powers to have on your side as you journey toward prosperity. But don't discount other ancestors who may step forward to lend a hand. Family members who have passed on want to see you and your family succeed and are often willing to contribute to your efforts here on the physical plane.

Just like working with ancestors for any other purpose, it is best to build a relationship with them before you start asking for favours. A small ancestor altar or collection of photographs where you can leave offerings and honour their memories is a great place to start.

Offerings:
Water, white candles, favourite food or drinks

Work with them when:
You are seeking anything. Your supportive ancestors are on your side when you are working to improve yourself and your life.

Disclaimer:
If you don't feel comfortable working with your ancestors, no one says you have to!

Budai (Laughing Buddha)

Though you might not recognize the name Budai, you are likely to recognize his other name – the Laughing Buddha. This is the joyful figure of a heavyset, smiling monk with a large belly that is depicted in countless statues around the world. He is often shown carrying a large bag that contains symbols of wealth such as money, food and treasure. In fact, his name means "cloth sack", in reference to what he carries.

Budai comes to us through Chinese folklore and Buddhist beliefs. A joyous and friendly figure, he often embodies contentment with one's lot in life as well as prosperity. If you rub his belly, you'll gain his blessings, resulting in prosperity and luck.

Offerings:

Incense, water, candles, flowers

Work with him when:

You are seeking a balance between material and spiritual contentment.

Cernunnos

A Celtic god of nature, fertility and wealth, Cernunnos is a powerful figure of wild and untamed nature. His antlered form reminds us that he is the Lord of the Wild, and therefore rules the cycle of growth, death and decay. As he is also related to the underworld, he is associated with precious metals and gems. Cernunnos is wild and primal in nature, and working with him requires a deep respect for the natural world. His influence can help you tap into the bounty of the earth.

Think of Cernunnos as a careful caretaker of resources who will help you learn to nurture your finances in a way that is respectful of the environment and the people around you. He will teach you lessons about sustainability and the cyclical nature of growth.

Offerings:
Fresh fruits and grains, antlers or bones, stones
and leaves, acts of conservation

Work with him when:
You want to enhance your connection to nature
to increase your wealth, or wish to ensure the
fertility or productivity of your projects.

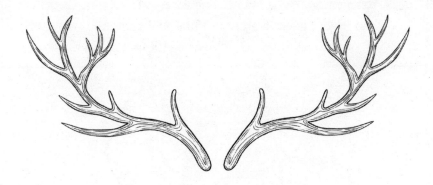

Hermes/Mercury

Both Hermes and Mercury are the famed messengers of their pantheons. Hermes belongs to the Greek pantheon, while Mercury is part of the Roman pantheon. Both are tasked with carrying information from one world to the next and both are psychopomps. However, they both also oversee things like travel, commerce and negotiations, elements that can play roles in your pursuit of wealth. Both gods are depicted as a young man with winged helmet and sandals, often shown carrying a caduceus. A winged staff circled by two twining snakes, the caduceus symbolizes skilled negotiation as well as the exchange and trade of goods.

Either Hermes or Mercury can help you cleverly negotiate a new raise or unite opposing sides in an argument for the benefit of all. Either can watch over you during business travel, ensuring your trip is not only safe but prosperous. As they are frequent travellers between this world and the next, they rule liminal states and transitions, so they can help you when you are trying to transition from one job to the next, move house or make other significant changes in your life.

Offerings:
Coins, olive oil, honey, cakes, representations
of the caduceus, acts of generosity

Work with either when:
You are negotiating important business agreements, need
to make a good impression while public speaking, or
need to talk someone into seeing things your way.

Jupiter

The Roman sky god and god of thunder, Jupiter is a powerful force. He was the ruler of the Roman pantheon and his attributes include lightning bolts, thunder and the Sun. He rules luck, money, expansion, material goods and generosity. While he is often considered the most powerful wealth god, some people also find him the most difficult to engage with. Not because he won't listen, but because his expansive nature tends to affect *everything*, including self-doubts or negative thoughts about money. For example, I have experienced him increasing my wealth by increasing the volume of my work! So if you decide to work with him, proceed with caution.

Jupiter is amazing at helping you make small things grow big. Think of building your bank account or taking a side business and turning it into your main money-making venture. Just be extremely clear when you are outlining what doesn't need to grow.

Offerings:
Sunlight, rainwater, gold-coloured items, acts of generosity

Work with him when:
You want to expand upon or develop a financial
situation that is already present and fairly healthy.

Lakshmi

The Hindu goddess of wealth, prosperity and beauty bestows material and spiritual riches. She is often shown standing on a lotus flower with gold coins falling from her hands. She is in charge of maintaining balance and prosperity in the universe. She rules wealth, fortune and the wellbeing of households.

Gentle and benevolent in nature, Lakshmi readily blesses those who seek her with sincerity. Her love of harmony means she enjoys residing in well-run, tidy households. She relishes order and regularity. If you can please her exacting tastes, she can bring you great abundance and sustained prosperity.

Offerings:
Fresh flowers (especially lotus flowers), fruits,
sweets, coins, jewellery, reciting mantras

Work with her when:
You want to increase the prosperity of your household while maintaining a balance between physical and spiritual wealth.

Saints

There are so many saints who are wonderful for money and wealth magic that it was hard to select just a few of them. I've written this section a little differently from the others because three of my favourites can be petitioned for help with very specific situations.

Saint Anthony – If you want to hold onto your job or stabilize your employment situation, he is your go-to saint! Burn brown candles in front of an image of him on Fridays and pray to him for help with keeping your job.

Saint Expedite – The patron saint of doing things quickly, he's your go-to for gaining small sums of money fast. Burn a red candle in front of him on a Wednesday and ask him for help getting the cash you need.

Saint Peter – If your living situation is unstable, burn brown or white candles in front of an image of him on a Saturday. He's known for carrying the keys to the kingdom, so ask him to lock you into your current home so you aren't forced to leave.

The Seven Lucky Gods (Shichifukujin)

The Seven Lucky Gods are a group of deities from Japanese folklore. They bring good fortune, wealth and happiness. Often shown gathered together on a treasure ship, especially during celebrations of the Japanese New Year, each god rules different aspects of fortune, and they work together to bestow a whole range of blessings.

Ebishu – The god of prosperity and abundant crops, a patron of fishermen. He is often shown with a fishing rod and a large fish.

Daikokuten – The god of commerce and trade, he is the patron of cooks, farmers and bankers. Also famed for his demon-hunting abilities.

Bishamonten – The god of warriors and protector of the righteous, he defends wealth and directs the righteous to treasures. He is often shown wearing armour and holding a pagoda and spear.

Benzaiten – The goddess of knowledge, art and beauty, she is the patron of creatives. She governs wisdom and talent, both of which can lead to wealth. She is often depicted playing a musical instrument, appearing with a *torii* or white snake.

Fukurokuju – The god of happiness, wealth and longevity, he is the patron of chess players. He is often shown with an extremely large head and walking with a cane.

Jurojin – The god of longevity and wisdom, he can help you have a happy life. He is shown carrying a staff and a fan. The scroll tied to the fan contains the lifespan of all living things. He is often accompanied by a deer, which is a symbol of longevity.

Hotei – The god of fortune and guardian of children, he brings contentment and happiness. He is shown dressed as a monk but with an exposed belly, and representations of him often include children. (If you think he sounds like Budai, above, you're correct!)

Venus

The Roman goddess of love, beauty and fertility, Venus's day of the week is Friday, which is traditionally considered payday in many parts of the world. Part of her domain is the wealth associated with relationships, fertility and the pleasures of life. She is depicted as a beautiful woman rising from the sea, a hint at her association with endless bounty. Her symbol often appears on the Empress card in the Tarot, reminding us that with fertility and growth comes abundant resources.

Venus represents harmony and attraction as well as prosperity, so she is a great ally if you are attempting to gain wealth through creative endeavours or through speaking or negotiations. Her influence can help you be more attractive and charming.

Offerings:
Roses, honey, beautiful things, pearls

Work with her when:
You wish to enhance your creativity or fertility, grow
your resources or improve your social connections.

THE GOLDEN GRIMOIRE

MONEY SPELLS

Use these spells to attract small amounts of money to help make ends meet, bolster your savings or achieve other small financial goals. These spells are all about simplicity and expediency, so they don't require a lot of components. The supplies they do require are easy to find and may already be in your home. I use spells like these to stabilize my finances in times of need. If I work with a spiritual ally while doing so, it's usually Mercury or one of my ancestors.

THE GOOD AND BAD LUCK OF TWO-DOLLAR BILLS

In the US, the standard currency denominations are $1, $2, $5, $10, $20, $50 and $100. This means that these types of paper notes are still printed by the US Treasury. There are bills with larger denominations and they are still useable, but the government doesn't print them any more. However, of all the paper money being printed in the US today, the most magically interesting is the two-dollar bill. Relatively rare, it doesn't usually make an appearance when you are given change. However, some folks like to go to the bank and exchange their money, so they have two-dollar bills to spend around town.

For those readers not in the US, you don't have to deal with two-dollar bills unless you choose to seek them out. However, if there is a coin or paper money denomination where you live that is treated similarly, the information below will likely apply.

When I was young, some folks went to the effort of carrying two-dollar bills and leaving them as a portion of the tips they gave, as they were not commonly seen. One afternoon I was at a fast-food restaurant and the person next to me paid for their meal with money that included a two-dollar bill. Imagine my surprise when the cashier saw the strange money in her hand and screamed before throwing it on the counter! She crossed her arms and refused to pick it up.

The man who was trying to pay for her food assured her that the money wasn't counterfeit, but she still refused to pick it up and put it in the till. Her manager came over to see what was happening and was sympathetic to her concerns. He scooped up the paper note and slipped it under the stack of singles in the cash register drawer so she could complete the transaction.

To say that my curiosity was piqued is an understatement. I was happy there was a large family placing their order in front of me. It gave me enough time to watch the manager murmur something into the cashier's ear while he reopened the till.

He picked up the offending bill and tore a tiny bit off one corner. Then he handed it to her so she could reluctantly do the same.

I wasn't bold enough to ask them what they were doing and why, but when I got home I asked my dad about it. He collected coins and some paper money so I figured he might have some idea of what they were doing.

Dad explained to me that while many people consider two-dollar bills lucky and carry one in their wallet to bring good fortune, just as many people seem to consider them bad luck. Lots of reasons have been suggested for the bad-luck belief, most of them circulating around two-dollar bills being associated with gambling, vote-buying and prostitution.

What Dad didn't know, and I found out much later in life, is there is another reason to be wary of two-dollar bills. They are often used as

THE GOLDEN GRIMOIRE

components in spells, and as you don't know what kind of spell a bill may have been used in, it is best to avoid them altogether.

If you encounter a two-dollar bill of dubious origin, you can avert any bad luck from the interaction by tearing off a tiny corner of the note and throwing it away. However, this solution becomes its own problem because it is illegal to deface US currency. What's a magician to do?

If you find a two-dollar bill in your wallet and want to ensure it doesn't adversely affect your financial luck or if you want to go to the bank and get one on purpose, here are some ways you can cleanse the bill without tearing it.

- Salt – This wonderful, all-purpose magical tool is perfect for absorbing and negating any disruptive influences that linger on a piece of paper money. Sprinkle a generous portion on a plate and lay the two-dollar bill on top of it. Then cover the bill with salt. Place your hands over the plate and speak your intent to the salt. Say something like, "Salt, creature of earth, banish, destroy and eliminate any and all negative influences from this money." Allow the bill to remain in the salt for at least an hour or overnight if possible. Then tuck the note in your wallet and spend it as soon as possible. Better yet, drop it in a donation box!
- A moon bath – During a full moon night, when the sky is clear, leave the bill somewhere where the light of the moon will shine on it. A well-positioned windowsill will do perfectly. If you must put it outside, make sure to weigh it down so an errant breeze doesn't solve your bad-luck concerns for you by passing the bill on to someone else! Ask the moon to carry away any negative influences.
- Cleansing with frankincense – Light a stick of frankincense incense or put some granules of frankincense resin on some coals. When there is plenty of smoke, run the bill through the smoke several times.

THE GOLDEN GRIMOIRE

TO TURN A TWO-DOLLAR BILL INTO A MONEY-DRAWING LUCKY CHARM

For those of you who don't live in the US, there are places online where you can buy a two-dollar bill. If you do, I still strongly recommend cleansing it, especially if you plan to use it for a charm like this one. Or if you have a type of currency in your location that is used in spell work, you can use that instead.

TIMING
Any time.

SUPPLIES
- A two-dollar bill
- Supplies for one of the cleansing methods above
- Abundant Wealth Oil (page 247) or olive oil

STEPS

1. Cleanse the two-dollar bill using one of the methods above.
2. Hold the two-dollar bill in both hands and picture what you want it to do (draw money, bring you financial gain, etc.). Make sure you can clearly see the results of your desired intent.
3. Tell the two-dollar bill what you want it to do. I usually say something like, "Special cash, draw money and draw it fast. Bring wealth to my wallet."
4. Dab a tiny bit of Abundant Wealth Oil (page 247) or olive oil on each corner of the bill and in the centre.
5. Fold the bill toward you twice.

USING THE TWO-DOLLAR CHARM

Tuck your new money-drawing charm in a small bag or in the back of your wallet. Make sure you carry it with you when you leave your house.

If you ever don't want to carry it, and you've constructed a wealth altar, you can store the charm there.

THE MAGIC OF
LUCKY COINS

There are a lot of simple good-luck charms out there that are said to ensure you will never have empty pockets. Many of them centre around carrying some type of lucky coin. There are plenty of beautifully designed coins that are made specifically as luck-drawing tokens. But you don't need to buy something if you don't want to. The following two methods are some of my favourites.

Carry an old coin

The magic of this practice is linked to consistency (carrying the good-luck charm every time you leave the house) and making a special effort (carrying a coin that can't pay for anything). Choose a coin that you find particularly appealing. It might be an old foreign coin from a trip you took once upon a time. Or you might buy an old coin at a thrift store or yard/boot sale. Whatever the case, I suggest choosing one that you can't spend where you live.

The creation of this lucky charm can be as simple or as complex as you wish. Just selecting the coin with the intent of carrying it to bring money your way is enough. Or you may wish to cleanse and anoint the coin, as in the two-dollar charm on page 179.

Whatever you choose to do, make sure to carry the coin with you whenever you leave your property. It's okay to carry it in a purse, wallet or backpack. It can even rattle around in your pocket along with your other loose change.

Handle it often, and when you do, take a moment to picture the money headed your way!

As with all money charms, if you can't carry it for one reason or another, you can store the charm in or on your wealth altar. If you don't have an altar, store it somewhere safe like a jewellery box.

Carry three pennies (or another coin of low value)

If you don't have a special coin you want to carry around, you can get the same results by choosing three pennies to carry with you wherever you go. Select three shiny pennies (or any low-value coins of the same denomination) to carry. If you can't find shiny coins, spend a little time polishing them. While you do, focus on all the money and prosperity your new charm is going to bring to you.

When I use this method, I put the coins in a small felt or gauze bag to keep them separate from the other coins in my purse.

Again, you can make the creation of this charm as simple or as complex as you want. If you want to cleanse and bless the coins or the bag, you can use the information on creating a two-dollar charm on page 179.

Any time you come across your special coins, reflect on the money they are drawing to you. And whatever you do, *do not* spend them!

COLLECTING (AND SPENDING) LUCKY SEVENS

Several years ago, I was at an open-air market and was thrilled to find a stall selling authentic charms and magical items from Mexico. After I selected several items and brought them to the proprietress to purchase, she was kind enough to explain how to use each one. I don't usually pay for things in cash, but I happened to have enough in my wallet to pay her. I felt moved to pay for my new magical goodies in cash and I am awfully glad I did!

After taking my money, the owner carefully examined one of the dollar bills I gave her. She shook her hand and gave it back to me.

"Do you have a different one?" she asked.

Taken aback, I pawed through my wallet for a different dollar bill. As I handed it to her, and fearing that I had picked up counterfeit money somewhere, I asked, "Is there something wrong with that one?"

She smiled at me, shaking her head, and said, "No, no – but you gave me one of your Sevens."

I must confess that I blinked at her in confusion.

Giving me a significant look, she said, "You know about the Sevens, right?"

"The Sevens?" I asked.

"Let me explain." She motioned me closer and ducked her head as though she was about to impart an important secret to me – and she did!

Up until that point, I had lived all my life not knowing that some dollar bills were luckier than others. When I first handed her the money, she had produced a stack of bills to make change out of her apron pocket. She pulled one from the bottom now and pointed at the Federal Reserve District number on the front side of the dollar. It was a seven. "This is lucky," she explained. "If you carry dollars with the sevens on them, you'll never go broke."

"What do I do with them?" I asked. "Just keep them?"

"You keep them separate from the others. You spend them last. But you must spend them, so that other people can get them, too. They bless you while you have them, then you bless someone else when you spend them."

It was starting to sink in. "That's amazing," I said.

She nodded. "Oh! And if you collect twelve, all with sevens on them, you take them out of your wallet and keep them somewhere safe. Then you'll *really* always have money. Here's another one so you can start."

She handed me my three dollars in change, making sure one of them was a Lucky Seven. "Now you have two so you can start your collection."

This interaction resulted in my entire family collecting and saving Lucky Sevens.

So if you are ever in the United States, keep your eyes open for Lucky Sevens and make sure to keep them!

Here is a summary of information about Lucky Seven dollar bills:

- Check the Federal Reserve number on the front side of the dollar note. If it is a seven, it's lucky.
- Keep the Lucky Seven dollar bills separate from the other cash in your wallet.
- The Lucky Sevens bless you while you have them, but you must spend them eventually to pass the blessing on to others. I like to include them as gifts in birthday cards for my friends who are in the know.
- There is one case where you should take your Lucky Sevens out of your wallet and keep them. That's when you manage to collect 12 of them, one for every month of the year.
- If you collect 12, keep them in a safe place where no one else can find them. As long as no one else touches them, they will draw wealth to you.

Though this specific practice is unique to US one-dollar notes, you can make this applicable to the money in your region. You may decide to keep coins with your birth year on them or paper notes with a serial number ending in a seven. The symbolism of the act remains the same and keeps you aware of your money and the blessings it gives you, and encourages you to pass those blessings on to others.

CALLING FOR A JOB

When job-seeking, one of the first things you should do is grab your phone and activate your friend and professional networks. "It's not what you know, but who you know" is a cliché, but for good reason! But in addition to calling around and asking for leads and introductions, you should also put the message out into the world on a spiritual level. There are two different approaches and both work well.

Approach 1

TIMING
Every night before bed.

SUPPLIES
- Five minutes of quiet

STEPS
1. Come up with a simple way to describe the job you are looking for. Example: "I want to find an office job that pays at least $25 an hour and is no more than a 20-minute drive from home."
2. Face east. Imagine you can feel a cool, fresh spring breeze on your face. Picture a placid meadow filled with flowers. Say, "Beings of the east, spread the word. I want to find [then state the description of the job you want]."
3. Face south. Imagine a dry, hot wind sweeping toward you. Picture a rough, red desert with a brightly shining sun. Say, "Beings of the south, spread the word. I want to find [then state the description of the job you want]."
4. Face west. Imagine the fine spray of a majestic waterfall hitting your face. Picture the waterfall plummeting into a deep pool. Say, "Beings of the west, spread the word. I want to find [then state the description of the job you want]."

THE GOLDEN GRIMOIRE

5. Face north. Imagine the deep, earthy smell of a cave. Picture a powerful mountain rising in the distance. Say, "Beings of the north, spread the word. I want to find [then state the description of the job you want]."

6. Turn back to the east. Say, "Send my message to the four corners of the world and bring me the job that suits my needs."

Approach 2

This method works great when you have established a relationship with an ancestor who is active and likes intervening on your behalf. It also works well if you have an ancestor that reminds you of prosperity or hard work.

TIMING

Once a week on Fridays for at least three Fridays in a row.

SUPPLIES

- 5–10 minutes of quiet
- A favourite beverage of your ancestor (water works fine if you aren't sure what they would prefer)
- White candles
- A picture of an ancestor you are close to (optional)

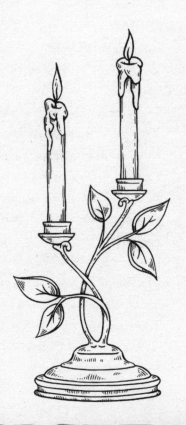

STEPS

1. Sit down somewhere comfortable with a picture of your ancestor (if you have it).

2. Offer them a drink.

3. Have a conversation with your ancestor about your current situation and what you need to accomplish. If you have worries about your finances because you are out of a job, tell them about it. If you fear that you aren't going to be able to support yourself or your family, tell them that, too! Pour your heart out. Talk to them just as if they were sitting there with you.

4. Ask them to help you find a job that will allow you to pay your bills and support your household. Thank them in advance for their assistance.

5. Spend 3–5 minutes listening in silence once you are done speaking. You may receive important messages from them. Don't forget that the messages won't necessarily be in words. You could feel physical sensations, experience memories or hear something that reminds you of important information.

6. Light the white candle as a thank you for their time. If you have a picture, light it in front of the picture. If you don't, light the candle on your wealth altar or in another safe place.

BRINGING ATTENTION TO YOUR APPLICATIONS

When paper applications and résumés were the norm, it was easy to sprinkle a little oregano for money, cinnamon for attention or mint for luck on the application after filling it out. Then I would tap the papers well to remove any sign of my magical activities. Now that most applications are submitted online, we have to be a little more creative.

TIMING
Any time you submit a job application.

SUPPLIES
- Personal prosperity sigil or other symbol of prosperity

STEPS
1. Before submitting your application, take a moment to close your eyes and picture yourself doing the job for which you are applying. See yourself working happily and well, with a satisfied boss who appreciates what you do.
2. Picture yourself receiving your paycheque and being delighted with the amount.
3. Point at the screen of the device you are using and trace your personal prosperity sigil or other symbol of prosperity over the screen.
4. Say, "A perfect match is what you'll be. Make it so that I am seen."
5. Then hit the submit button.

A CHARM BAG TO HELP YOU ACE ANY JOB INTERVIEW

It's rare that you'll find a person who loves going to job interviews. It's a high-stress experience in which you are determined to present your best and most marketable self. You also never know what kind of questions to expect. In addition to going into the interview prepared by practising answering questions and learning as much as possible about the company, you can carry what I carried at every job interview, whether it was in person or online.

TIMING
Wednesday during the waxing moon or any time you need it.

SUPPLIES
- A small green felt bag (approximately 5x5cm [2"x2"])
- Lemongrass essential oil
- Cinnamon
- Oregano
- Lemongrass
- Cinquefoil/Five-finger grass
- Red pepper
- Citrine
- Pyrite
- Salt
- Incense (sandalwood or your favourite scent)

STEPS

1. Put the incense in the holder and light it.

2. Put a generous pinch of salt in the bag, close it and shake the bag to distribute it around the inside. Say, "Creature of earth, cleanse this bag so that I may use it for my magical purposes." Open the bag and dump out the salt.

3. Sprinkle another pinch of salt on each side of the bag, repeating the words from step 2. Shake the salt off the bag.

4. Fill the bag with smoke from the incense and pass the bag through the smoke several times. Say, "Creature of air, cleanse this bag so that I may use it for my magical purposes."

5. Put several pieces of lemongrass in the bag. Say, "Lemongrass, open the channels of communication between me and everyone I speak to. Let them see me in the best light. Bless my tongue so that I am heard and understood."

6. Put a pinch of oregano in the bag. Say, "Oregano, bring me money through this job. Bring this prosperous opportunity to fruition."

7. Put a pinch of cinnamon in the bag. Say, "Cinnamon, let my passion and dynamic nature shine through, to the appreciation and acceptance of all."

8. Put a pinch of red pepper in the bag. Say, "Red pepper, fire me up. Energize me with enthusiasm and determination."

9. Put a pinch of cinquefoil in the bag. Say, "Cinquefoil, show off my expertise and further the unfolding of my career."

10. Put a chip of pyrite in the bag. Say, "Pyrite, stone of wealth, let my voice be heard and let this interview lead to money."

11. Put a chip of citrine in the bag. Say, "Citrine, be the stone on which I build my career. Let the way open so this job is mine."

12. Tightly close the bag.

13. Pass the bag through the smoke of the incense. As you do, picture yourself dazzling your interviewers. See yourself receiving a generous job offer afterwards.

14. Before your interview, put four drops of lemongrass essential oil on one side of the bag and five drops on the other (nine drops in total).

THE GOLDEN GRIMOIRE

USING THE BAG

If you are going to an interview in person, carry the bag with you in your pocket or purse. Just before you meet with your interviewers, squeeze the bag so a little bit of the lemongrass oil gets on your hand. If you are interviewing online, hold the bag out of sight throughout your interview.

FOUND MONEY BRINGS MONEY

There is an important concept in money magic that found money will attract more money to it (and to whoever found the money). So while many people may say, "Find a penny, pick it up, and all day long you'll have good luck", we magicians might say, "Find a penny, pick it up with glee, and watch as money flows to thee!"

Now, many folks think you shouldn't pick up a coin if it isn't heads up. That doesn't apply in this case. Pausing to pick up a coin or bill is a message to the universe and to your subconscious that you honour and are receptive to every bit of good fortune that comes your way. It is a demonstration of both humility and practicality.

If you see money on the ground, you might wish to say something as you pick it up. I use the rhymed saying above, but you could also say something like, "As I pick up this penny, there is more wealth coming my way."

What should you do with found money? If you've created a wealth altar, give it a special place there to honour it. If you don't have an altar, put it in a safe place where you store things you treasure. After you've had it in your possession for a while (a week to a month), you can spend it or pass it on to someone else who needs a little jolt of financial luck. If you know a bunch of magically minded folks, coins like these can circulate for months or even years, carrying more significance and power the longer they are preserved and passed on.

HIDE A NICKEL IN A HOLE TO KEEP YOUR POCKETS FULL

This short, sweet little spell can be worked on the spur of the moment and doesn't need many supplies. The purpose of this spell is to ensure you never have empty pockets. You can even work it more than once, but it shouldn't be worked in the same place twice. It is easiest to do this one while you are travelling because once you perform the spell, you are not supposed to ever return.

A nickel is a US coin that is worth five cents. You can use a nickel for this spell or another coin that is worth five of something. Or you can use any small-denomination coin you have on hand – because who would want to pass up this opportunity just because they don't have a nickel?

TIMING
Choose a time when you are in a place you won't be coming back to. This doesn't have to be a far-flung location, just a place to which you are unlikely to return.

SUPPLIES
- Ideally a nickel, but any small coin will do
- Something to dig with (a pointy stick, a spoon, etc.)

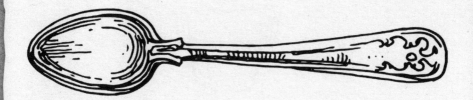

STEPS

1. Pick a spot that appeals to you but that won't disrupt or disturb the scenery or other people.

2. Using your digging tool, dig a shallow hole.

3. Put the nickel/coin in the hole and cover it well. Make sure it is completely hidden.

4. I usually ask the nickel to keep my pockets filled. You can do this or skip this step.

5. Stand up, turn around and walk away without looking back.

6. Don't ever return to the location.

MAKE SURE YOU DON'T
GET UPROOTED

When money is scarce, there is a higher risk of losing your beloved home. Whether you might need to move to find a better job or downsize due to cash-flow issues, being forced to move is never pleasant. This spell helps prevent you from needing to worry about money and being forced to move as a result.

TIMING
Any time, but I like doing this spell on a Sunday.

SUPPLIES
- A bottle (I prefer glass, but a sturdy plastic bottle will do)
- Honey (enough to fill at least half the bottle)
- Brown sugar (enough to fill a quarter to a third of the bottle)
- Clingfilm
- Tape

STEPS

1. Clean the bottle if necessary. Clean it physically first. If you desire, wash it with blessed water or fill it with incense smoke to cleanse it spiritually.

2. Scoop brown sugar into the bottle. As you do, picture your landlord (if you're a renter) or bank (if you have a mortgage) being kind to you. See them being flexible and understanding of your issues, and treating you sweetly. You can speak your desires to the sugar at that point and tell it what you want it to do. Fill the bottle until it is a quarter to a third full.

3. Pour honey into the bottle. Make sure not to spill one drop. As you do, picture yourself being flush with cash and able to pay all your bills. Picture yourself secure and relaxed when it comes to money. Fill the bottle until it is two-thirds to three-quarters full.

4. Tightly cap the bottle. Shake it gently to combine the brown sugar and honey.

5. The bottle must be stored upside down, so make sure the bottle will not leak. You can wrap the end of the bottle in clingfilm or tape to ensure it remains sealed.

6. Take the bottle to your bedroom and flip it upside down. Store it that way under the head of your bed under the left-hand side. If necessary, use tape to secure the bottle to the leg of your bed so it doesn't fall over.

7. When I have this spell going, I spend a little time each night after I get into bed reinforcing it. Focus on sweetness and understanding coming from people who are in positions to help you, including your landlord, bank, employer and members of your support system.

MONEY MAGNET SPELL

This spell will draw money to you from all directions, providing you with a steady and abundant flow of cash. It is based on the idea of building a small model of the universe which you then symbolically manipulate so that money comes to you.

Though it may seem complex, it really isn't. And its concrete, physical components are a great help to folks who might struggle with visualization.

This spell works best when you can set the scene and leave it undisturbed as you work the spell from day to day. If you don't have enough space, you can try making a smaller version that will allow you to let it remain standing over the course of the full eight days of the spell.

TIMING

Prepare for the spell on a Thursday. The spell itself starts on a Friday and lasts seven days (so eight days in total).

SUPPLIES

- Five strong magnets (I like using large disc magnets that look like coins)
- Paint markers
- A compass
- A green marker
- A large white piece of paper
- A gold candle
- A silver candle
- Two candleholders
- Personal prosperity sigil (optional)
- A small green bag (that can hold all the magnets)

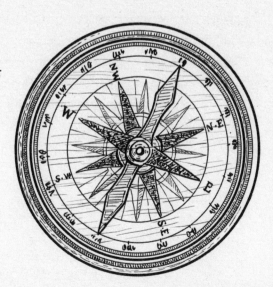

SETUP

Follow the steps below to set the scene for this spell. Do this on a Thursday (day 1). What you are ultimately doing is constructing a micro-universe you can symbolically manipulate so that money comes your way.

1. Prepare the magnets.
   - Using a white paint marker, write your initials on one of the magnets. This magnet will represent you.
   - Using paint markers, decorate the other four magnets to look like gold coins. These magnets will represent all the different ways money might come to you.
2. Prepare the paper.
   - On the large white piece of paper, use a compass to sketch a large circle.
   - Use the green marker to trace the circle.
3. Place the candles on the paper.
   - The gold candle symbolizes the Sun. Put it in a candleholder and position it to the right of the large circle.
   - The silver candle symbolizes the moon. Put it in a candleholder and position it to the left of the large circle.
4. Place the magnets on the paper.
   - If you are using it, put your personal prosperity sigil in the centre of the circle, face up.
   - Put the magnet that represents you in the centre of the circle.
   - Put the magnets representing money around the edges of the circle, one in each of the cardinal directions.

THE SPELL

Starting on Friday, do this every day for seven days (days 2–8):

1. Light the gold candle representing the Sun. Say, "Let the golden rays of the Sun shine down on me, bringing abundance and wealth."

2. Light the silver candle representing the moon. Say, "Let the silver rays of the moon shine down on me, bringing prosperity and plenty of money."

3. Touch the magnet in the centre of the circle representing you. Say, "I name you [your name], recipient of abundant wealth and endless prosperity."

4. Move each of the four magnets symbolizing money about one-seventh of the way closer to the centre of the circle. As you move each magnet, say, "Money from all directions, from sources known and unknown, all and only for the greater good, come to me."

5. Let the candles burn for 30 minutes. While they burn, picture yourself being the recipient of money and experiencing prosperous situations. For example, see yourself receiving a bonus, obtaining an unexpected sum of money, or selling your products if you run your own business.

6. Extinguish the candles.

7. Leave everything as it is until the next day.

8. Repeat steps 1–7. Eventually, the magnets will get so close to each other that they will join. If it happens early (before day 7), don't worry about it. Take it as a sign that approaching money is even closer than you think!

Complete the spell:

9. On day 8, the magnets should all be joined together. Put the joined magnets in the green bag.

10. If you used a copy of your personal prosperity sigil, put it in the green bag too.

11. Store the green bag in or on your wealth altar or in another safe place.

MONEY-DRAWING
SHAKER BOX

This magical little box is used to call money to you. It is simple to make and doesn't require expensive components. It is excellent to use in a pinch when you need a small amount of cash. Once you make it, you can use it every day. Store it in a dresser drawer or on your wealth altar.

TIMING
Any day or time will do!

SUPPLIES
- A small box (I like to use a large matchbox or a small gift box)
- Green paper (or paper you can colour green)
- Markers, crayons or coloured pencils
- Glue or tape
- Dry rice or beans
- Coins

STEPS

1. The first step is to make the outside of the box green. I find it easiest to trace the sides of the box on green paper and cut them out. Then I glue them to the box. Make sure the box can still open. You could also paint the box green with markers or crayons.
2. Decorate the inside and outside of the box with symbols that represent money to you. You can draw money bags, safes, treasure chests, coins, paper bills or signs for the currency you are trying to attract. As you draw, picture the box being a magnet for money. (If you have created your personal prosperity sigil already, draw it inside the box.)
3. Put a small handful of rice or dried beans in the box while saying, "Many and many and many more. Bring money in my door."
4. Put a small handful of change in the box while saying, "Like to like, bring your friends, so my cash flow never ends."
5. Close the box and seal it with the glue or tape.

USING THE BOX

Whenever you feel worried about your finances, pick up the box and give it a good shake, saying, "Many and many and many more, bring money in my door. Like to like, bring your friends, so my cash flow is without end."

You can also create your own chant to suit your needs.

PROTECT
EXPENSIVE ITEMS

When you are working your way out of debt or trying not to live paycheque to paycheque, replacing or repairing an expensive item like a car or home appliance can set you back months. This simple visualization is something you can do regularly to build a wall of protection around the things that make your household run smoothly. It's brief, so you can choose to do it daily or weekly. I like to do this right before I go to bed at night.

TIMING
If you do this weekly, do it on a Tuesday.

SUPPLIES
- About 5–10 minutes of quiet

STEPS

1. Get physically comfortable in a chair or lying down.
2. Close your eyes and take deep, calming breaths. Release the tension from your body and see it draining out of the soles of your feet and palms of your hands.
3. One at a time, picture each item. See it as clearly as you can in your mind's eye. Allow it to rotate in front of you so you can see all sides of it. Visualize a golden glow surrounding the item so that it is protected and secure.
4. Picture the item happily working inside its golden shield.
5. When you are finished with the first item, move on to the next. I prefer starting with my most important item (it used to be my car so I could get back and forth to work).

It is important to note that working with household possessions like this often stirs up activity from any household spirit that dwells with you. If it does, and you start noticing items being moved or going missing, it means that they are reaching out to you to provide some assistance. Leave out some gifts for them (fresh water, milk, bread or honey). Don't leave these gifts on your wealth altar. Place them on your kitchen table overnight or at your back door. The next day, pour them out on the ground. As you build a relationship with these spirits, you can start asking them to help protect your home and belongings.

HEALTH PROTECTION POMANDER

Health problems make it difficult to earn and manage money. Whether your family's health concerns are acute or chronic, they can reduce your energy levels and make it difficult to earn money. Though no magical charm can defend you and your family from all the medical maladies that could come your way, it never hurts to reinforce your household's health with a charm that can help build a wall of defence against illness.

This pomander charm has the dual benefits of being aesthetically pleasing and being linked to a historical practice that was used to preserve health. We are just going to add a few magical features to reinforce its effect. The orange and all the herbs that are used have protective and money-attraction properties. As you create the pomander, you can speak charms and make wishes for the health of your family. You can also visualize and meditate on how you want to protect your family from health issues and concerns.

Like all magic, this method works best with physical, real-world efforts like maintaining a healthy diet, a good sleep schedule and regular visits to healthcare professionals.

TIMING
Any time.

SUPPLIES
- Oranges (one per pomander)
- Whole cloves
- Powdered cinnamon
- Powdered allspice
- Powdered nutmeg
- Powdered Queen Elizabeth root
- Red cloth ribbon (or any other colour you prefer) – optional but recommended

- A nail, skewer or toothpick
- Rubber bands
- A soft graphite pencil
- Straight pins
- A small bowl
- Paper bags big enough to fit an orange (one per pomander)

STEPS

1. Wash and thoroughly dry the oranges.
2. Plan the design. You might wish to stud the entire orange with cloves or you could outline magical signs of protection with them. (The more cloves you use, the better the chance of the pomander drying out thoroughly without moulding.)
3. For each pomander, wrap the ribbon around an orange, crisscrossing it as if it were a present. Tie the ribbon firmly and leave a long end at the top of the orange for hanging. (Use the pins to hold the ribbon in place if it keeps slipping off before you can tie a knot in it. You can either use pins with decorative heads and leave them in the ribbons or remove them once the ribbon is secure.)
4. When you have tied the ribbon, hold the orange in your hands. Say, "Blessed sphere, symbol of the Sun, shine your blessings on all in my household."
5. Using the soft graphite pencil, sketch the design you planned in step 2 on the exposed parts of the orange. Wrap the rubber bands around the orange if you want guidelines for making straight lines.
6. Use a nail, skewer or toothpick to pierce holes in the orange skin. In this step, you are pre-drilling the holes for the whole cloves. I like using an iron nail for this step as iron is an excellent metal for protection. During this process, picture your family remaining healthy and happy.
7. If there is any graphite left from your guidelines, gently wipe it off with a paper towel.
8. Once the holes have been pierced, select some whole cloves and press them into the holes you made so that the rounded end of the clove

is the only part sticking out of the orange. During this process, say, "Cloves, nature's nails of protection, drive away illness and discomfort."

9. When all the cloves have been inserted into the orange, mix the powdered spices in a small bowl. Use about a tablespoon of each herb per orange.

10. Put the hand you write with over the bowl and say a blessing over it. Say something like, "Spices of protection and wealth, bless my family with a wealth of good health."

11. Put the pomander ball in a paper bag. Put a liberal amount of the powdered spice mixture in the bag. Roll the pomander around so it is thoroughly coated.

12. Leaving the spices and the pomander in the bag, close the bag with the ribbon extending out of it. Fasten it with pins.

13. Hang the pomander from the ribbon in a place with good air circulation and allow it to dry. Let it dry for a few weeks. The cloves draw out the juice, so the oranges will shrink in size. Cinnamon is an antifungal, so its presence helps prevent moulding. Open the bags every few days to check them and make sure they aren't moulding. If one moulds, throw it away and start over. (This is why I like drying them in separate bags. If one moulds, it won't spread to the others.)

14. When the oranges are light and sound hollow when tapped, they are fully preserved. Remove them from their bags and dust off any extra spice mixture.

15. Hang the pomanders as a protective decoration in your home.

Your preserved health protection pomanders will last a long time. However, if they ever lose their scent, you can refresh the spell by mixing a few drops of clove, cinnamon and orange oil and anointing the pomander with the mix. As you do, repeat the charm from step 10 and picture your family remaining happy and healthy.

SIMPLE WAYS TO TURN YOUR LUCK

Sometimes, it feels like no matter which way you turn, you hit a brick wall. When you first start digging yourself out of financial difficulties, you might feel like there is no way out. If your frustrations are running high and you are down on your luck, it can be difficult to stick to your plans. When this is the case, it is time to turn your luck. There are several different ways to do this. Here are two simple practices that can help lift your spirits and get you back on track.

TIMING
Any time you feel stuck or unlucky.

Method 1: Salting Your Wallet

SUPPLIES
- Your wallet
- Salt (any kind will do)
- A tray big enough to hold the contents of your wallet
- Incense that is bright and astringent-smelling

STEPS
1. Take everything out of your wallet.
2. As wallets can be catchalls, especially when our lives are busy, make sure to throw out any trash/unnecessary paper. Make sure you dispose of any unnecessary business cards, particularly any that might be weighing you down or projecting negative influences. If you need the information from the card, put it in another safe place. Don't keep it in your wallet.
3. Pour enough salt into the tray to cover the bottom of it. Tell it to absorb and destroy any disruptive influences that are getting in your way.
4. Put the contents of your wallet that you want to keep into the tray.

Note: If you have made any magical charms and kept them in your wallet, set them aside. Do not put them in the tray.

5. Put your wallet in the tray also.
6. Sprinkle a liberal amount of salt over your wallet and its contents.
7. Open your wallet and put several pinches of salt inside.
8. Light the incense.
9. Circle the tray counterclockwise three times, saying, "Turn my luck and take it back, get me on the right track."
10. Let your belongings sit in the salt for at least 15 minutes, longer if possible.
11. Carefully empty the salt out of your wallet and dust the salt off your belongings.
12. Reassemble your wallet. Take your time. Do it with thoughtful intent, with the knowledge that doing so is turning your luck and getting things back on track.
13. Dispose of the salt.

THE GOLDEN GRIMOIRE

Method 2: A Healing Spin

SUPPLIES
- A cup or small bowl
- Fresh water
- Salt

STEPS
1. Put three generous pinches of salt into a cup or small bowl of water, saying, "Creature of earth, cleanse this water and make it fit for my purposes."
2. Stir the water counterclockwise, saying, "Creature of water, bless and cleanse all you touch."
3. Put the prepared water somewhere safe.
4. Stand up and turn counterclockwise three times. (Or if you have an office chair, remain seated and spin the chair counterclockwise!)
5. As you spin say, "Twist and turn and clear my way, my luck is reborn today."
6. As soon as you stop spinning, grab your water and bless yourself with it. At minimum, dip your fingertips into the water and dab some on your forehead, the back of your neck and the palms of your hands. Take your time. If you feel other areas need your attention, bless them with the water too.
7. Clap your hands briskly three times and know that your luck has turned!

TRIPLE-LUCK MONEY-DRAWING POWDER

This powder can be used in your home or your business to draw money. The three herbs used in this mixture all draw luck, but each one also contributes its own unique influences. The instructions call for dying the cornstarch green, but this is optional. I suggest dying the powder because if you leave it white, it stands out when you sprinkle it on the floor. This recipe makes a lot of powder, so you can make up a batch and share it with your friends.

TIMING
Make this powder on a Wednesday when the moon is waxing.

SUPPLIES
- Half a cup of cornstarch
- Green food colouring – or colour of your choice that represents money
- Cinnamon (powder or oil)
- Nutmeg (powder or oil)
- Clove (powder or oil)
- A jar with a tight-sealing lid
- A baking sheet
- Water

STEPS
PREPARATION – DYING THE CORNSTARCH
(Do this part in advance. It can take up to two days for the cornstarch to dry.)

1. Put one cup of cornstarch in a bowl.
2. Mix in up to half a cup of water. You want the mixture to be the consistency of thick glue. You might need less than a half-cup.
3. Add several drops of food colouring and stir until the colour is evenly distributed throughout the mixture. The number of drops you need will depend on how deep you want the colour to be and how effective your food colouring is, so you will need to experiment until you are satisfied. Remember that the colour will lighten once the cornstarch dries.
4. Spread the cornstarch in a thin layer on the baking sheet. The thinner the layer, the more quickly it will dry out. Put the baking sheet in a warm dry place and let it sit for up to two days.

THE SPELL
1. After two days, check the moisture level of the powder by rubbing a pinch or two between your fingers. Unless your environment is exceedingly dry, the powder will probably still be damp.
2. If your powder needs to dry out more, preheat your oven to 350 degrees Fahrenheit. Once your oven reaches that temperature, turn it off. Put the tray of powder in the oven. Let it sit for 30 minutes and then check the moisture level.
3. When the cornstarch is dry, remove it from the oven and let it cool.
4. Once the cornstarch is cool, crush it to remove any lumps. You can use a mortar and pestle or the back of a large spoon. (If you want to do it quickly and easily, put it in a clean food processor or blender.)
5. When the cornstarch is prepared and you are ready to make the powder, prepare yourself.
6. Prepare your magical working space.
7. Put the dyed cornstarch in a jar with a tight-sealing lid, saying, "Colour of wealth and growth, carry my intentions to the four corners of the world."

8. Add the oils/herbs.
   - When you add the cinnamon say, "Lucky cinnamon, your constant warmth stimulates positive opportunities and opens the way for money to flow my way."
   - When you add the nutmeg say, "Lucky nutmeg, you always draw abundant wealth to me."
   - When you add the cloves say, "Lucky cloves, you turn away disruptions and usher in wealth."
9. Put the lid on the jar and shake it to mix the powder together. While you shake the jar, picture yourself receiving money from a variety of sources: paycheques, royalties, online sales, refunds, gifts, and whatever other ways money could find its way into your hands.

USING THE POWDER

- Incorporate the powder into the popular method of blowing cinnamon into your front door on the first of every month to welcome money into your home.
- Carry a pinch of the powder in your wallet or purse, or dust the inside of your handbag with it.
- Sprinkle the powder in manifestation bowls or encircle candles with a ring of it.

PROSPERITY SPELLS

These spells are great for expanding your wealth once you have a stable foundation. They can help you eliminate bad habits that might threaten that stability. They can also assist you to build on and grow your wealth. Some of these workings are reactive because they help solve problems you already have, but a good deal of them are proactive because they help you maintain what you have and improve upon your existing situation.

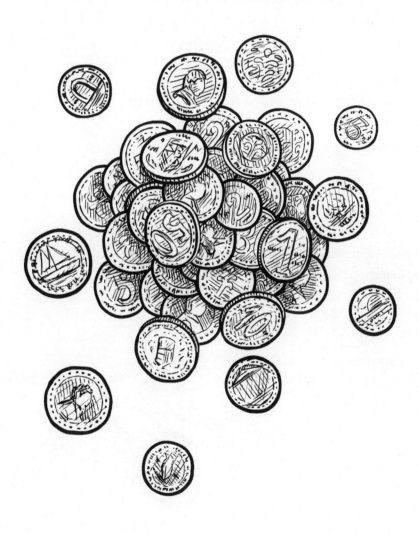

ASK FOR A RAISE

Even when you are doing an excellent job at work and you know you are being underpaid, it is always difficult to put yourself forward and ask for a raise. However, working for less than you are worth doesn't just negatively impact your bank account. It can have a detrimental effect on your self-image and contribute to feelings of burnout and frustration. Eventually, you may find yourself resenting your job, unwilling to give it your full effort. If you are considering asking for a raise, here is a spell that can help swing things in your favour.

TIMING

The night before you plan to ask for your raise, a Wednesday if possible.

SUPPLIES

- Paper
- A pen or pencil
- A Mercury dime or small picture of Mercury
- A yellow candle
- A candleholder
- Lemon, lavender or sandalwood incense
- An incense holder
- Two pieces of hard candy (I usually use lemon, because it's a favourite flavour of mine)

STEPS

1. Give your Mercury dime or picture of Mercury a place of honour on your desk or workspace.

2. Put the yellow candle and incense in front of the image of Mercury. Light them saying, "Lord Mercury, bestow your blessings on me. Help me to think with clarity and speak with grace."

3. In bold block letters at the top of a page, write "ARGUMENTS FOR MY RAISE". Underneath that, list all the reasons you believe you deserve a raise. Be thoughtful and thorough but don't exaggerate. List facts like work you do above and beyond your job description, the number of years you've been with your company, and your reliability.

4. Gaze at the image of Mercury and say, "Lord Mercury, I need and deserve a raise. I leave my arguments with you. When the time is right, bless my mind with clarity and sweeten my tongue so my request is approved. If I get my raise, I'll give you [an offering – I usually promise more of the hard candy]."

5. Leave both pieces of hard candy in front of the image of Mercury until the candle and incense burn out. (You can extinguish the candle if necessary, but allow it to burn at least as long as the incense.)

6. On the day you are going to ask for your raise, bring your paper listing your arguments, the image of Mercury and the candies to work with you in your pocket or purse.

7. Immediately before you go to ask for your raise, read the list of arguments (if you can't openly read it, just hold it for a few moments and mentally review what you wrote on it). Then put one of the candies in your mouth. Say (or think), "Lord Mercury, now is the time. Bless my efforts."

8. When you finish eating the candy, it's time to switch on your confidence and go ask for that raise!

BANISH BAD
SPENDING HABITS

No matter how much money you bring in the door, you will never reach financial equilibrium and be able to save for the future if you don't control your spending. There are many different things that cause people to spend when they shouldn't: boredom, impulse, feeling celebratory, or just being unable to wait to get what they want. Whatever prompts you to spend when you shouldn't, this spell can help you get that under control.

TIMING
During the new moon (when the moon is dark and can't be seen in the sky).

SUPPLIES
- A small white candle
- A small black candle
- A small dish
- Two pieces of paper (approximately 6x6cm [2.5"x2.5"])
- A pen
- Long tweezers

STEPS
1. Think about what causes you to spend money when you shouldn't. It may be difficult to think about, so take your time and really dig into the causes, and the situations that make it too easy for you to spend money you don't have or that is earmarked for other purposes. This might require doing some journalling or using some other form of self-reflection to understand the details. Some questions to contemplate:
   - Is your overspending related to your emotional state?
   - Are you troubled by impulse buying?
   - Are you more likely to overspend when you are out with friends?
   - Do you fall prey to temptation when you shop online?

- Does it happen when you have extra cash in your wallet or when you have access to a credit card?

2. When you feel ready, use one piece of paper to record what causes your bad spending habits. Use words, pictures or a combination of both. You can write things like "BOREDOM", draw a group of stick figures spending money, or sketch the logo of a website where you do most of your shopping. Take your time and put it all down. This process in itself can be cathartic.

3. Fold the paper in half. Write "BANISH" on the outside of the paper with firm pressure.

4. Fold the paper in half again. Write "DISSOLVE" and "DESTROY" on the outside of the paper with firm pressure.

5. Put the paper in a dish. Hold the black candle in the hand you write with and say, "Colour of the dark moon, dissolve and diminish my bad habits, seal them away so I am left untouched."

6. Light the black candle and carefully drip wax all over the paper. Once one side is dry enough, flip it over and drip wax all over the back. Cover the front and back entirely. You may need to use the tweezers to manipulate the paper so you don't get burned by the hot wax. Set the paper aside to dry.

7. Clean the black wax out of the dish and dispose of it in the trash.

8. Think about the good money habits you want to cultivate. It may be that you want to stop and think twice before you spend, or you might want to commit yourself to sticking to your spending budget.

9. Use the second piece of paper to record those good habits that you want to sustain and carry with you at all times. Use words, pictures or a combination of both. You can write something like "Think twice" in fancy script or draw the word "BUDGET" with supports propping it up.

10. Fold the paper in half. Write your full name along with your date of birth on the outside of the paper.

11. Fold the paper in half again. Write "DEVELOP" and "GROW" on the outside of the paper with firm pressure.

12. Put the paper in the dish. Hold the white candle in the

hand you write with and say, "Colour of the growing moon, support my growth and development."

13. Light the white candle and carefully drip wax all over the paper. Once one side is dry enough, flip it over and drip wax all over the back. Cover the front and back entirely. You may need to use the tweezers to manipulate the paper so you don't get burned by the hot wax. While you do, picture yourself doing the things you recorded on the paper. Set the paper aside to dry.

14. Hold the paper with the habits you want to banish in the hand you write with. Hold the paper with the habits you want to attract in your other hand. Close your eyes. Feel the opposing forces that you hold.

15. Move the hand holding the bad habits away from you. Say, "This I discard."

16. Move the hand holding the desired good habits to your heart. Say, "This I retain."

17. Dispose of the bad habits. You can do this by burning the wax-covered paper if you feel comfortable doing so. Make sure to do it in a well-ventilated place and over a non-flammable surface. If you choose to do this outdoors, be aware of the wind and minimize burning embers. In other words, take all precautions to keep yourself safe. (I usually do this step over my kitchen sink with the window open. I hold the paper in a long pair of tweezers.) If you don't want to risk burning the paper, throw it away in a trash can that is not in your home or place of work/business.

18. Keep the good habits talisman you prepared in your wallet with your money. (You can wrap it in plastic to avoid crumbled wax getting all over your wallet or purse.) Keep it in a place where you have to see or preferably touch it before you access your money. If you usually shop online, keep it in a place in your home where you usually shop. Before making a purchase, consciously open yourself up to its influence and let it help you make the right decisions. Each time you use the talisman successfully, it grows in power.

BLESSING YOUR MONEY-MAKING TOOLS

If your livelihood depends on specialized tools, you know the havoc that can be caused when those tools break or are lost. A musician can't play with their instrument, a delivery person can't deliver without their vehicle, a tarot reader can't divine without their deck. If you consider your livelihood an artform, you probably also have a sentimental attachment to the tools of your trade. I have a deep love not only for the tarot and oracle decks I use but also for the electronics and reference materials that allow me to write. This spell helps keep your beloved and valuable tools safe and sound.

Sometimes when working on a valuable item, our techniques can be limited because we don't want to damage the item. For example, I can't really bless my favourite tarot deck with magical water without being exceptionally careful. Or there are times the item is too big to easily work with. This spell uses a blessed miniature that can remain safely on your wealth altar. If you don't feel the need to use a stand-in item, you can perform this spell with the actual tool.

This spell requires you to put things near open candle flames. Please use caution when working with an open flame. If you aren't comfortable doing so, use the smoke of cleansing incense instead.

TIMING
A Thursday during a waxing moon.

SUPPLIES
- A miniature of the item you want to bless (or a picture or description of the item)
- A black candle
- A white candle
- A candleholder
- Water

- Salt
- A bowl
- A white or black bag

STEPS

1. If using a miniature or picture, hold it in the hand you write with. Place your other hand on the actual item. Say, "One and the same, always the same. As I act on one, so it is done to the other."
2. Close your eyes and see the two items – the actual item and the miniature – melding together to become the same thing.
3. Put the black candle in a candleholder and light it. Say, "Let your light banish and drive away all bad luck, difficulties, dangers and threats that this [item name] encounters from now until forever."
4. Pass the miniature over the flame of the black candle.
5. Picture the actual item being cleansed and cleared of any and all disruptive influences.
6. Extinguish the black candle.
7. Light the white candle. Say, "Let your light bless and protect, so this [item name] works perfectly and reliably and does not fail from now until forever."
8. Pass the miniature over the flame of the white candle.
9. Picture the actual item being surrounded in a golden-white glow of protection.
10. If you are using miniatures, store them in a white or black bag. Keep the bag on or in your wealth altar, or in a safe place like a jewellery box or your closet.

BLESSING YOUR MONEY
(SO IT BLESSES YOU
AND EVERYONE ELSE)

When working for my financial development, I find I often get amazing results when I work on the behalf of others at the same time. Generosity of spirit and the accompanying positive power it puts out into the world is extraordinarily effective at drawing all types of abundance to you. This spell blesses your money, so it finds its way back to you when you spend it. But the money also blesses all those it touches with a little bit of abundance magic. You can use this working to bless cash, credit cards, gift cards or anything else that represents value. As the representation of the money (paper bills and coins, digital transactions, etc.) changes hands, it brings good luck and prosperity to you and the recipient as well as anyone else that handled the transaction (bank tellers, cashiers, wait staff). You can even work this spell on a bag of low-denomination coins and sprinkle some wherever you go, letting the power of abundance bless an entire area.

Note:
You can do this spell on your wealth altar or in
any place you have the space to work.

TIMING
This spell can be done at any time, but Wednesdays are a good day for it.

SUPPLIES
- Representations of money (e.g., the cash in your wallet, your credit or debit cards, your savings account statement)
- A green candle (or any candle representing prosperity – *see* "The Colours of Wealth" on page 143 for more information)
- A candleholder

- A drawing of your personal prosperity sigil (optional)
- A bowl
- Salt
- Abundant Wealth Oil (page 247), or another money/prosperity essential oil

STEPS

1. If you are working with your personal prosperity sigil, place a drawing of it face up in the centre of your workspace.
2. Put the bowl in the centre of your workspace (on top of the sigil if you are using it).
3. Place the candle in its holder and position it on the far side of the bowl. Light the candle and say, "Glowing beacon of abundance, guide my actions so that all may be blessed by what I do."
4. Put a pinch of salt in the bottom of the bowl and say, "Creature of earth, banish any disruptive influences from the contents of this bowl."
5. Put in some of your money/representations of money.
6. Repeat steps 4 and 5 until all the money/representations of money you wish to include are in the bowl. Sprinkle a final pinch of salt on top.
7. Pour a few drops of Abundant Wealth Oil into the palm of your hand. Dip your finger into it and anoint the entire rim of the bowl with the oil. As you do, say, "Blessed oil of abundance, let the spending of this money bring more money. Let the exchange of this money bless all it touches, physically and metaphorically. Let this money bring money back to me."
8. Relax and picture the money you send out into the world returning to you and bringing more back with it. See it blessing everyone it interacts with and bringing them peaceful prosperity along the way.
9. Place your hands over the bowl. Holding an image of your intent in your mind, say, "As you go, you will grow, blessing all you meet. As you return, I will earn, increasing my balance sheet."
10. Leave the money in the bowl so that it can absorb as much wealth energy as possible. Allow the candle to burn out or burn for at least two hours.

THE GOLDEN GRIMOIRE

BURYING TROUBLE

What's a witch or magician to do when they just can't kick a bad habit? Maybe it's overspending or forgetting to pay your bills. Perhaps you have a hobby that consumes too much of your money or time, but you find it impossible to stop. You might even be haunted by a destructive thought that damages your confidence or irritates your wealth wounds. Here's a simple method I use when I must put a stop to something fast. I like it because you can customize it to meet your needs.

TIMING
When the moon is waning on a Saturday.

SUPPLIES
- Black paper
- White paper
- A white gel pen or marker
- A blue or black pen
- A stapler
- A place to bury your work

STEPS
1. Prepare a paper coffin. As you do, focus on the fact that you are constructing the final resting place of your bad habit.
    - Using the black paper, cut out two coffin shapes that are the same size. It can be a plain rectangle, or you can cut out an old-fashioned coffin shape, whichever you prefer.
    - Using the white gel pen, draw a cross on one coffin shape. This is the top of the coffin.
    - On the other coffin shape, use the white gel pen to write, "The death of [insert bad habit]." Write boldly. This is the bottom of the coffin.
2. Prepare the body.

- Write a description of your bad habit on the white paper. Include as much detail as you like.
- Make sure to write about your frustrations and the difficulties the bad habit causes.
- Fold the white paper describing your bad habit so it is smaller than the black coffin-shaped papers.

3. Lay your bad habit to rest.
- Place the bottom of the coffin on your workspace, writing side down.
- Place the written description of your bad habit on top of it.
- Put the top of the coffin on top of the stack. The white paper shouldn't be visible.
- Say, "This is the death of [bad habit]. It will live no more. It will not return and will not haunt me."

4. Drive in the nails of finality.
- Using the stapler, staple all around the edges of the coffin to seal it. As you do, see yourself driving nails into the coffin.

5. Bury your bad habit for good.
- In a secluded space, dig a shallow hole. If you are doing this on your property, make sure it is an out-of-the-way place. If you are on someone else's property, make sure you have permission.
- Put the coffin in the hole and cover it with dirt, tamping it down firmly by stepping on it with your foot.
- Cover the bare dirt with leaves, grass or other natural materials so that it blends in with its surroundings.
- Walk away without looking back, feeling your liberation.

FABULOUS AND FASCINATING

Every now and then, I'm faced with a situation that requires me to dazzle someone (or sometimes a whole room of people). I might be pitching the idea for a new project, talking to a client or presenting a class. When I worked in the corporate world, there were times I needed to ask for a raise, give a tricky presentation or attend an important meeting. There were also times when I felt I wasn't getting the attention I deserved for the work I was doing. How does a witch stand out from the crowd and keep everyone's interest? This spell is one that has worked for me more times than I can count. It occasionally needs to be reinforced throughout the day. However, sometimes it works a little *too* well and it takes a while to wear off. A soak in a tub with Epsom salts helps to ground the energy and bring back equilibrium.

TIMING
While you are getting ready to go to the meeting/give the presentation/put on a show.

SUPPLIES
- A favourite piece of clothing, accessory, item of makeup or perfume/aftershave
- A mirror

STEPS

1. Once you are ready to put on whatever is going to be the focal point of your spell, hold the item in the hand you write with.

2. Look at your reflection in the mirror. Make and maintain eye contact with yourself.

3. Picture yourself being the fabulous and fascinating person you know you are. See yourself saying the right thing at the right time, knowing exactly what to do at each point, listening actively and talking vividly. See everyone's positive reactions.

4. When you have the picture firmly in your mind, say, "Fabulous and fascinating, fabulous and fascinating, fabulous and fascinating to all who see me."

5. Repeat the charm in step 4 twice more (so that you say it three times in total). On the third time, lift the item that is the focal point of your spell, so it breaks your eye contact with your image in the mirror. Make sure you move it so you can no longer see the reflection of your eyes.

6. Put on the item, knowing it will highlight all your best features whenever anyone sees you or hears your voice.

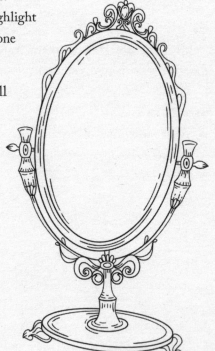

As mentioned above, this spell works best when you reinforce it throughout the day. From time to time, take a moment to repeat, "Fabulous and fascinating, fabulous and fascinating, fabulous and fascinating to all who see me."

KEEP A JOB/ CONSTANT WORK SPELL

Sometimes, even having a job isn't enough to make you feel financially secure. We have all been in situations where it feels like we could lose our jobs at any moment. When you aren't sure if you will stay employed, it's hard to plan for the future. Ever heard the term "busy as a bee"? This spell uses bee symbolism to help stabilize your work situation. It can help you keep the job you have or help you maintain a steady flow of clients if you do freelance work.

TIMING
This work can be done at any time. If you plan to perform this work several times in a row, do it once a week on Friday evenings or whatever day you get paid.

SUPPLIES
- A picture of a busy beehive (this can be a drawing, something you print off the internet, or a copy from a book)
- A shallow dish
- A small mug
- A spoon
- A beeswax candle
- Honey
- Warm milk
- Your company's logo (or your name if you are freelancing)
- Personal prosperity sigil (optional)

STEPS
1. Light the beeswax candle. Say something like, "Light from the fruits of consistent labour, illuminate this spell and give me steady work."
2. Prop up the picture of the beehive behind the dish. Say something like, "Friend bees, support my efforts."

3. If using your company's logo, write your name on top of the logo. (You don't have to do this step if you are freelancing and using your name.)

4. Put your company logo/your name in the dish, face up.

5. If you are using your personal prosperity sigil, place it on top of your company logo/your name.

6. Warm up the milk (just enough so it will dissolve the honey).

7. Put about a tablespoon of honey in the bottom of your mug. Say something like, "Let the sweetness of this honey be the sweetness of my boss's/clients' thoughts of me."

8. Fill the mug with warm milk. Say something like, "May my boss/client be filled with the milk of human kindness and may they look favourably on me."

9. Stir the milk and honey mixture clockwise. As you stir, visualize yourself excelling at your work and your boss/client taking notice. Picture the results you want.

10. Drink the honey-sweetened milk, reserving a sip or two of it. As you sip, meditate on the honeybee, the concept of work, and how you can work in a healthy way to support yourself and your family. Think about what makes work sweet for you (even if it is something as simple as getting that paycheque every week)!

11. Pour the reserved milk and honey mixture into the dish on top of your company's logo. Say something like, "Sweet and steady my work will stay."

12. Place the candle in the centre of the dish on top of your company logo/name and prosperity sigil.

13. Allow the candle to burn out or burn for at least an hour. If you don't burn the whole candle, you can save it for the next time you work this spell. You can leave the saucer with the milk and honey in it on your wealth altar for a short time, but make sure to dispose of the contents of the saucer before the milk sours.

WORKING WITH ST TERESA OF AVILA TO HOLD ONTO YOUR JOB

In addition to the spell described above, St Teresa of Avila can help you keep your job. If you are comfortable working with a saint (and remember, you don't have to come from a religious faith that recognizes saints to work with them), purchase a St Teresa medal and wear it. As long as you wear the medal, your job should be secure.

If you want to further improve your chances, use a picture or statue of St Teresa. Put the representation of the saint on your wealth altar or in a location central to your home. Offer her gold, red or pink candles. Give her fresh water and roses. Petition her to help you keep your job by writing your request on a piece of paper and putting it in front of her image.

PAMPERING YOURSELF TO GET IN TOUCH WITH YOUR PROSPERITY

When working magic to improve your financial situation, it can be difficult to put yourself in a prosperous and luxurious state of mind. Whether you are struggling to make ends meet, fairly comfortable or even flush with cash, it is a challenge to genuinely recognize and feel how fortunate you are. There are always problems and concerns that get in the way of acknowledging your blessings.

This active meditation is one that will evoke feelings of luxury, allowing you to express your gratitude in a systematic and magical way. It centres around giving yourself a conscious self-care session so you can count your blessings and express gratitude for what you have.

Choose whatever type of self-care makes you feel the best. It may be a long, relaxing bath or a home facial or a night on the couch with a blanket, snacks and a favourite movie. Choose something that you thoroughly enjoy but that you don't often indulge in. Whatever you choose doesn't need to be expensive. Do this when you can set aside enough time to genuinely enjoy every moment. You don't want to feel hurried or anxious to get through this.

TIMING
Whenever you can set aside enough time to indulge in the decadent pampering session of your choice.

SUPPLIES
- A small stone or charm you can use as a focus item. It should be something you can carry with you easily during and after this ritual. You can use a drawing of your personal prosperity sigil if you don't have a charm or stone you like.
- Any items you need for your pampering session

THE GOLDEN GRIMOIRE

STEPS

1. Set up your pampering session. This might entail going to a salon or spa or setting up your living room for a quiet night of reading. Take your time to make things special.

2. Make sure you have your focus item with you.

3. Before the session begins, clap your hands three times, and say, "And so it begins!" (If you are going out for a coffee or to a spa, you can do this in the car or subtly do it outside before you walk in.)

4. Begin your relaxation/luxury session. Allow yourself to sink into it and really enjoy the feeling of being pampered.

5. Once you feel thoroughly relaxed and happy, start listing all the things that are making you happy or comfortable. If you're by yourself, do it out loud. If not, do it mentally.

6. For each thing you identify, squeeze or rub your focus item and think about why or how you have this thing that makes you happy. Examples:
   - This popcorn. I can buy it because of my job.
   - This time to focus on myself. I can indulge this way because my partner is watching the kids.
   - This blanket. I have it because my best friend gave it to me for my birthday.
   - These chocolates. I have them because the little store down the street carries them.

7. Spend as much time as you can enjoying your self-care session and being present with the sensations that make you feel pampered.

8. At the end of your pampering session, hold your focus item and make a statement of gratitude. You could say something like, "All the things I identified are blessings I acknowledge. I appreciate them and treasure them. I know my blessings will grow over time."

9. Carry your focus item with you, especially on days you are feeling burned out, tired and hopeless. Let it be a reminder of all you already have and all the good things that will be coming to you in the future.

PROSPEROUS HOUSEHOLD SEVEN-DAY CANDLE

This candle can be burned on a wealth altar or anywhere else in your home. It is fast and easy to prepare with simple supplies that you likely already have on hand. I use bayberry-scented candles when I can find them because, as the saying goes, "A bayberry candle burned to the socket brings joy to your life and money to your pocket." You can choose a candle colour based on the colour of the currency where you are, or you can select a colour based on the information in the "Colours of Wealth" section on page 143. This is a wonderful technique to use when there are multiple money-earners in a household, and you want to bless and support all of them.

While you can buy glass-encased candles that are specifically made for attracting wealth, they are usually much more expensive than plain green candles. When I am at my frugal best, I prefer to work with the plain candles as any preparation work I do will be more powerful than a design printed on the glass.

> **Note:**
> This method DOES NOT include putting crystals in the wax well of your candle. This is an extreme fire hazard because heat can cause crystals to explode. Never burn a candle with a crystal in the wax well.

TIMING
This method works at any time. Wednesdays, Fridays and Sundays are all great days to prepare your candle.

SUPPLIES

- A glass-encased seven-day candle
- Metallic gold and silver paint pens (or green permanent marker)
- A black felt-tipped pen or fine-point permanent marker
- Triple-Luck Money-Drawing Powder from page 210 (optional)
- Salt
- Bay leaves
- Mint
- Camomile
- Basil
- Pine or other cleansing incense
- An incense holder
- A lighter

STEPS

1. Before you get started, decide on a primary intention for your candle. It should be something you can sum up in a word or two. Some examples are "prosperous household", "steady work" or "abundant money".
2. Prepare yourself.
3. Prepare your workspace.
4. Clean the candles physically and spiritually.
    - Physically – wipe down the glass with a damp towel, dust off the top surface of the candle
    - Spiritually – Light some incense and run the candle through the smoke with the intention of removing all influences from it
5. Using gold and silver metallic pens, decorate the glass of the candle. Use single words and short phrases that support your intention. For example, "steady cash", "constant cash flow", "savings", "new opportunities". You can also include wealth symbols like currency signs and your personal prosperity sigil.
6. Place the candle on a safe surface.
7. Encircle the candle with salt. Though salt is often used to purify and bless items, this time it is being used to represent wealth so

that it can draw more of the same to it. You can also use Triple-Luck Money-Drawing Powder (page 210) to encircle the candle.

8. Mix a small amount of dried mint, camomile and basil.

9. Put three tiny pinches of the herb mixture on the top of the candle, where the wax well will be, saying, "Camomile for abundance, mint to attract, basil for luck."

10. Summarize your intention and write it on a bay leaf with the black pen. Put the prepared bay leaf in front of the candle.

11. Burn the candle for an hour or two every day. Watch the candle carefully as there are powdered herbs in the wax well.

SPRINKLE SOME SALT TO IMPROVE YOUR SALES

If you run your own business or sell at events, you have likely noticed that there are people who leave a heavy energy behind them after they visit your place of business. They could just be having a bad day, but their mood lowers the energy of their surroundings. This influence often slows things down, which can have a negative impact on your shoppers and your sales. If you want to correct the problem quietly and simply, make sure to keep some salt and a broom on hand. Salt is an excellent and inexpensive magical tool that absorbs and clears away disruptive influences. For this practice, any type of salt will do, including salt you get out of a packet from a restaurant.

When you want to improve the energy of your store or vending stall, sprinkle some salt on the floor, telling it to absorb any energy that is disrupting your sales. Let it sit on the floor for a few minutes. Then briskly sweep the salt away. Sweep it all the way out the door, if possible. If you can't sweep it out the door, sweep it into a dustpan and dispose of the salt in a trash can.

TO MAKE SURE YOUR VOICE IS HEARD: THREE LITTLE PIECES OF GOLD

When I worked in the corporate world, it was in a male-dominated field. There were many times it seemed I couldn't get the attention of my team or my managers, even when I knew I had the solution or expertise to solve a problem.

Not only is it frustrating when your expertise is ignored or your contributions aren't recognized, it can also have a detrimental effect on your job performance and your career. This is an effective and subtle spell that you can use in any work environment. It serves as both a reminder and a confidence booster to allow you to speak up despite your current work environment, and increases the chances of your voice being heard.

Several friends of mine have tested out this easy spell, and they all reported great success.

TIMING

This spell is more powerful if worked on a Wednesday when the moon is waxing.

ENTITIES TO WORK WITH

Depending on your preference, any one of these entities can assist you with this magical work.

- An ancestor you work with regularly and/or who represents financial stability or expertise
- A god or goddess that represents communication, like Mercury or Iris
- The patron saint of your professional field

SUPPLIES

- Three small pieces of pyrite (fool's gold)
- Two small gold or yellow candles
- Glitter (choose a colour that best represents your personality)
- A small bag or box (optional)
- An image or representation of any entity you wish to work with (optional)
- Salt
- Water
- Personal prosperity sigil drawn on a piece of paper (optional)

STEPS

1. Place the two candles on a fire-safe flat surface about 20cm (8") apart.
2. Put a piece of paper decorated with your personal prosperity sigil or other prosperity symbol between the candles.
3. Light the candles.
4. Take a pinch of salt, and tell it something like, "Cleanse and bless all you touch."
5. Put the pinch of salt in the water and say something like, "As this salt blesses you, become my tool for cleansing all you touch."
6. Wash all three pieces of pyrite in the blessed water. Don't dry them off.
7. Place the pyrite between the two candles, on top of your prosperity symbol.
8. Sprinkle three pinches of glitter on the pyrite, one on each stone. As you do, say something like, "May my knowledge shine through in every situation. May my voice be heard."
9. Summon up an image of yourself being heard and your messages being received clearly and favourably at work, in meetings and conversations.
10. Hold the image in your mind. Embody the experience. Feel how nice it will be when people listen up. Channel your intention, vision and feelings into the pyrite. As you do, repeat this three times:
    I shine. I gleam.

> *By all I'm seen.*
> *I speak my words*
> *By all I'm heard.*

11. If you are working with an entity, pray or speak to them
    to request they add their assistance to your efforts.

12. Leave the pyrite undisturbed for an hour or until the candles burn out.

13. If you are planning on keeping the pyrite as a charm,
    gather up the pyrite, prosperity symbol paper and
    some of the glitter, and place them in the bag.

Bring the pyrite stones to work and keep them there, if possible. Depending on the nature of your work environment, you might:

- Put just the stones on your desk or workstation
- Put the bag or the stones in a drawer you use often
- Put the bag in your locker
- Carry the bag with you in a pocket or around your neck

I kept pyrite that was prepared in this way on my desk. If I had an important meeting to go to, I'd grab one of the three stones and put it in my pocket and take it with me.

In my experience, I didn't have to recharge this spell over the course of several years. If you want to recast it at any time, just take the pyrite home and follow the steps above.

If you change jobs (and especially if you change careers), cleanse the pyrite in salt water and recast the spell, visualizing yourself communicating successfully in your new role or position.

I have been asked by one conscientious practitioner if they could use real gold instead of pyrite. Of course you can! Three small pieces of gold will work just as well as fool's gold. If you use real gold, keep it in a bag and carry it with you.

WEALTH SPELLS

These wealth spells open up a world of financial opportunities. There are spells here that you can turn to when you are applying for loans, looking for financial advisors, and capitalizing on property or prospects you already own. Most of these spells are proactive. They are about looking to your future and ensuring you continue to make good financial decisions. Except for the Anti-Evil Eye spell that begins this section, I often work with Jupiter when performing these spells.

ANTI-EVIL EYE

The concept of the Evil Eye is a complex one, but the most important things to know are that it is caused by jealousy and that it is often *not* intentional. However, when you are working hard and making progress on your goals, the eye of envy could easily fall on you. Projects and people are always more vulnerable to the Evil Eye when they are in transition. When you are working to get out of debt, improve your finances or set yourself up for a wealthy future, you are putting yourself in a space of transition and growth. Early attempts could be thwarted by disruptive influences from the Evil Eye. The Evil Eye is known to cause spiritual sickness, bad luck, bad moods and accidents. As your household conditions improve, you may draw attention that might do you harm. What's a wise witch to do? Follow the steps below to protect yourself, your home and your property.

Personal protection

The easiest way to protect individuals from the Evil Eye is wearing a protective symbol on your person at all times. Eye charms, horn charms and hamsas are all designs famous for protecting the wearer from problems caused by the Evil Eye. Choose a charm that appeals to you and select a comfortable way to wear it. Though I usually wear mine around my neck, there are times I pin it inside my clothing, or even pin it to the inside of my handbag. I always wear my protective symbol, even when I sleep and shower. So you may wish to consider picking a charm that can stand up to daily wear and water.

If you would like to protect your loved ones, gift them with protective charms and explain their significance. Then it is up to them to decide if they wish to wear the charm or not. For small children, you can give them a safe piece of jewellery to wear, but I prefer tying a small piece of black thread to their clothing and pinning a protective charm to their strollers.

If the charm or the method of attachment (chain, silk cord, safety pin) breaks, that means that the charm has done its work by absorbing disruptive influences. If the charm itself breaks, dispose of it respectfully by wrapping it in white material and burying it or placing it in a trash receptacle. Be sure to thank it for everything it has done for you! If the method of attachment breaks, dispose of it. Then clean the charm by holding it under running water or burying it in salt. Get a new chain or pin and your charm will be ready to protect you again.

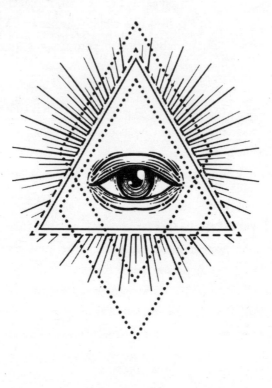

PROTECTING
YOUR HOME

The Ruler of the House spell on page 271 is one that can help you set a household to rights if it is suffering from the Evil Eye. But you may never need to perform that spell if you protect your home from its disruptive influences. Here is a fast and easy way to do that.

TIMING

Traditional Evil Eye protection methods don't require specific timing. However, I like to do work like this on the full moon or the first day of the month. I refresh these kinds of spells regularly, so doing it on a day that is easy to remember helps me to maintain them.

SUPPLIES

◖ Salt (any kind – table salt, coarse salt, pink salt, black salt)

STEPS FOR FREESTANDING HOMES YOU CAN WALK ALL THE WAY AROUND (WITH OR WITHOUT FENCES)

1. Take a large container of salt outside.
2. Take a large pinch of salt in the hand you write with, and tell the salt to keep your house free from the Evil Eye and all disruptive influences.
3. Turn to your left and begin to walk around your house, sprinkling the salt as you go. You don't need to make a thick visible line – just a sprinkling will do.
4. Continue talking to the salt and sprinkling it as you walk all the way around your house and back to where you started. Picture your home and household being protected and running well.

TIPS:

- I often do this late at night. It's much easier to do when you don't have to stop to explain what you are doing to your neighbours!
- When you talk to the salt, it doesn't have to be out loud. You can just say it in your head.
- If you have a fence that interrupts your circle, ask for help from a friend. Explain what to do and station them at the fence line. Start making your circle of salt around your home. When you come to the fence, hand the salt over the fence to your friend so they can complete the circle for you. (If the fence is too high, give them their own supply of salt at the beginning.)

STEPS FOR APARTMENTS, CONDOMINIUMS OR OTHER DWELLINGS THAT AREN'T FREESTANDING

This method can work even if your domain is a small room. Or you can apply it to an entire apartment or multi-level condo.

1. Stand in the centre of your space. Pick up your salt and walk to the boundary of it.
2. Take a large pinch of salt in the hand you write with, and tell the salt to keep your house free from the Evil Eye and all disruptive influences.
3. Instead of sprinkling a line of salt inside your house, you'll just be throwing a small pinch in each corner of your dwelling. Move counterclockwise as you do. When you are finished with each room, put a small pinch of salt in the centre before moving on to the next one. You may wish to put a small pinch on each windowsill and in each closet as well.
4. Continue talking to the salt and throwing pinches of it in the corners until you get back to where you started. Picture your home and your household being protected and running well.

Protecting your property

The methods used in "Protect Expensive Items" on page 202 and "Blessing Your Money-Making Tools" on page 219 can be applied to any item. Another way to protect physical items is to scratch or somehow disfigure them in an inconspicuous spot. Think a small scratch on the back of your TV or the underside of the new keyboard you just bought. Incorporating an imperfection into an item makes it impervious to jealous looks and envy. The scratch doesn't have to be big or deep and it doesn't have to be visible. Another way to make your beloved possessions "imperfect" is to spit on them. If you don't want to scratch an item, lick your thumb and rub some spit onto it! Whether you use the scratch technique or the lick technique, make sure to do it with the intention of protecting your items from the Evil Eye.

BLESSING YOUR TILL
OR CASHBOX

If you run your own business or are planning on selling merchandise at a yard sale or craft event, you can get more cash flowing your way through the time-honoured practice of blessing your till. There are many ways to do this, but this one is my favourite.

Note: Even if most of your sales are online, you can still do this spell! If you have an online business, follow these steps to create a symbolic cashbox which you can use for this work.

1. Print out the logo for your bank account. Choose the bank account where the money from online purchases is deposited.
2. Cut out the logo and tape it to the top of the box with waterproof tape.
3. Say, "This is and will be the physical representation of [name your account]."

If you do this, make sure to take care of this little box! Keep it in a safe place, and don't let it get dusty or neglect it – because it is now associated with your account and therefore your financial success. If you ever want to break the association, remove the bank logo from the box and wipe the box down with salt water.

TIMING
If you only sell things occasionally, do this the night before you plan to sell. If you run a store, once a week on Friday mornings is the best time, but any time on Friday will do.

SUPPLIES
- A cashbox/till
- A small bowl
- Salt

- Water
- A clean white cloth
- A lemon
- Incense (money-drawing or frankincense)
- Malachite
- Peridot
- Red coral
- A small bag
- A candle (green or the colour of the currency you'll be doing business in)
- A candleholder
- Personal prosperity sigil drawn on paper (optional)
- Packing or duct tape (if choosing to use personal prosperity sigil)

STEPS

1. Using the small bowl as a container, make some blessed water.
   - Pour about half a cup of spring or tap water into the bowl.
   - Add three big pinches of salt, saying, "Creature of earth, bless and cleanse all you touch."
   - Add a squeeze of lemon juice, saying, "Cleansing lemon, purify all you touch."
   - Holding your hands over the bowl, visualize pure white light gathering between your hands and direct that light into the bowl, saying, "This blessed water will clean all it touches, driving away all disruptive influences."

2. Dip the white cloth into the blessed water and wipe down your cashbox, starting with the inside. Make sure to clean every part. Focus on the fresh scent of the lemon and picture the blessed water banishing any influences that could distract customers or turn them away.

3. Allow your cashbox to air-dry, or dry it with another clean white cloth.

4. Light the incense and waft smoke all over your cashbox, inside and outside, saying, "Steady customers come to me, ready with cash in their hands."

5. If using a personal prosperity sigil, flip your cashbox over and tape the sigil to the bottom of it. Tape it so the side with the drawing faces the bottom of the box (the blank side of the paper should face you). Use strong tape like packing or duct tape. Take a moment to visualize yourself cheerfully helping a steady stream of happy customers.

6. Wash the pieces of malachite, peridot and red coral in the blessed water. Pat them dry.

7. Pass the malachite, peridot and red coral through the incense smoke, saying, "Turn paying customers my way, let them come night and day."

8. Put the stones in the small bag.

9. Put the bag of stones in a safe place in your cashbox where they won't get in the way. They should stay in your cashbox until the next time you perform this spell.

10. Put your candle in its holder. Place it near your till. Light it and say, "As you burn, infuse this box with the power to draw happy paying customers that I can serve best."

11. Let the candle and incense burn themselves out.

TO REFRESH THE SPELL

1. Empty out your cashbox, including the bag of stones. You can leave your personal prosperity sigil taped to the bottom. Just be careful when you wipe down the outside of the box with the blessed water, so you don't soak the paper.

2. Perform steps 1–11 above.

ABUNDANT WEALTH OIL

While there are many different herbs that can draw money, improve your financial situation and perpetuate wealth, my favourite is oregano. In addition to its ability to attract money, it is also famed for its ability to clear away disruptive influences and bring happiness. It takes centre stage in this Abundant Wealth Oil, which you can make to use in your magical work.

I usually make this oil with just oregano, but you can add other herbs to customize it to your liking. For example, you may wish to add a drop or two of patchouli oil to boost its ability to help you manifest your goals, or crumble some bay leaves into it to help with your career. *See* page 158 for a short list of money magic herbs.

TIMING
I like to start making this oil on a bright, sunny, Sunday.

SUPPLIES
- Oregano, fresh (a large bunch) or dried (four tablespoons)
- Olive oil (enough to cover the oregano)
- Salt
- A glass jar with a tight-sealing lid
- A deep pot
- Water
- A fine sieve or cheesecloth
- Additional herbs (optional)
- A small piece of pyrite (optional)

STEPS

1. If you are working with fresh oregano, strip the leaves from the stems, clean them thoroughly under running water, then pat them dry. You may wish to do this a short time before you make the oil so you can leave the oregano out for a while to air-dry.

2. Bruise or chop the oregano to help release the oils from the plant. If you are using fresh oregano, chop it. If you are using dried oregano, bruise it by crushing it with the back of a spoon or by using a mortar and pestle.

3. Carefully physically clean the jar you will use.

4. Spiritually cleanse the jar by putting three pinches of salt in the jar and one pinch in the lid. Swirl first the jar and then the lid, saying, "Powerful mineral of the earth, dispel all influences on this jar, leaving it ready for my work."

5. Place the oregano in the jar, saying, "Blessed herb, do your work for me. Draw wealth and happiness and drive away disruption."
(At this point, if you want to include any other herbs, add them to the jar with a statement about what you want each one to do for you.)

6. Pour the olive oil over the oregano until it is completely covered, saying, "Golden sign of prosperity, draw all good things to me."

7. Gently stir the mixture clockwise. As you do, envision all the things you want the oil to bring to you.

8. Put the lid on the jar.

9. Fill the pot with enough water so that when the jar is placed in the pot, the water will cover the contents of the jar but will not reach the lid.

10. Put the pot on the stove and heat it until the water is boiling.

11. Turn off the heat, leaving the pot on the burner.

12. Gently place the jar in the centre of the pot. Again, the water should cover the jar up to the contents, but it shouldn't reach the lid.

13. Leave the jar in the pot for 15 minutes (or longer – the longer you wait, the cooler the water will be and the easier it will be to get the jar out of the pot).

14. When at least 15 minutes have passed, carefully remove the jar from the pot.

THE GOLDEN GRIMOIRE

15. Check the lid to make sure it is tight. If it's not, tighten it again.

16. Dry off the jar.

17. If the sun is in the sky, hold the jar up so you can see sunlight shining through it. Say, "Let the golden rays of the Sun, source of all that is good, bless this oil and strengthen it day by day."

18. Place the jar on a sunny windowsill for 14 days. Shake the jar every day, and while doing so envision all the wonderful things the oil will draw to you. Say, "Draw abundant wealth and happiness with every use."

19. After 14 days have passed, pour the oil mixture through a sieve or some cheesecloth to strain it.

20. Store your Abundant Wealth Oil in a clean new container with a tight-fitting lid. If you choose, you can put a small piece of pyrite or other wealth-drawing stone in the container. Keep your oil in a cool, dark place.

WAYS YOU CAN USE THIS OIL

- Anointing candles
- Blessing magical jewellery
- Offerings to ancestors, gods and goddesses, and other entities
- Anointing your work area
- Putting a few drops in your bathwater
- Blessing your wallet or purse
- Blessing your wealth altar

BANISHING PAPERWORK PANIC WITH CALM, COURAGE AND CLARITY

Throughout your journey to wealth and financial abundance, paperwork will occasionally rear its demanding head. Whether you are filling out a form online to open a new bank account, registering a new business or filing your tax returns, you will eventually need to tick all the boxes and answer all the questions. Or you might even be faced with applying for a loan or incorporating your business!

Someone very near and dear to me doesn't just hate paperwork. When the paperwork involves something good, it makes them exceedingly nervous, and they often put off doing it until the last minute. When the paperwork is even more stressful, they really struggle with sitting down and getting it done. Throughout our friendship, I've always been ready to help them when it is time to file taxes or manage other official forms and documents. Because we can all get a little nervy when things get official, I've also developed this candle magic spell to help calm their nerves and keep them focused.

TIMING

Any time paperwork looms is the right time for this spell! If the paperwork is going to be filled out at home, prepare and light the candles before you start. If it is going to be completed in public, burn the candles before you leave the house. (Don't forget to make sure they are fully extinguished before you leave!) You could also have someone you trust light and tend the candles while you are out of the house completing the task.

LOCATION

Even if you have an altar to do magical work on, I find this spell works best when you burn the candles in the room where the paperwork is being done. If you can position them in a safe place on the desk where you will be working, that would be ideal. But any safe place in the room will work.

SUPPLIES

- An orange candle
- A light-blue candle
- A candle to represent the person suffering paperwork panic (choose a colour that appeals to the person for whom the spell is being worked)
- Three candleholders
- A toothpick or skewer
- Olive oil
- A lighter or matches

STEPS

1. Prepare yourself.
2. Prepare your space.
   Special note on your space: If you are going to be filling out something on paper, make sure to keep the form somewhere safe so you don't get anything on it while you work.
3. Gather your supplies.
4. Using a toothpick or skewer, carve the name and birth information of the spell's target (whoever is suffering from paperwork panic)

on the candle that will represent them. Use the individual's birth name, or magical name if they have one. Include their date of birth or some astrological information (for example, their Sun sign).

5. Dip your finger in the olive oil and rub it on the candle, saying, "I name you [name of person the candle represents]." To anoint the candle with the oil, start in the middle and rub the oil from the middle to the tip of the candle and then from the middle to the bottom of the candle.

6. Put the white candle in its candleholder.

7. Using your carving tool, carve the word "COURAGE" into the orange candle. If you choose, you can also carve some symbols that mean courage to you. While carving, speak to the candle and tell it what you want it to do. You can say something like, "Orange candle, draw in courage for [name], help [name] face this task."

8. Put the orange candle in its candleholder. Place it to the right of the white candle.

9. Using your carving tool, carve the word "CALM" into the light-blue candle. If you choose, you can also carve some symbols that mean peace and calm to you. While carving, speak to the candle and tell it what you want it to do. You can say something like, "Blue candle, bring [name] peace and clarity."

10. Put the light-blue candle in its candleholder. Place it to the left of the white candle.

11. Light the white candle first, saying, "[Name], as this candle is surrounded by courage, calm and clarity, so you shall be."

12. Light the light-blue candle next, saying, "Creature of fire, surround [name] in calm and clarity. Let it fill their mind."

13. Light the orange candle next, saying, "Creature of fire, surround [name] in courage and confidence. Let it fill their mind."

14. Allow the candles to burn as you fill out your paperwork.

BLESS YOUR BUSINESS CARDS OR OTHER PROMOTIONAL MATERIALS

If you have a business or need to promote yourself, you probably have business cards, flyers, or other materials you hand out to advertise your business or services. Or you might have a job that requires the use of a business card. Either way, it can be hard to get the right kind of attention today, because we live in a world of constant distractions and split focus.

I have been perfecting my personal brand's style for years, but I didn't see a lot of success until I started blessing my business cards.

If you want to improve your business prospects, use one of the methods below to bless your cards and/or advertising materials. I strongly suggest you test out your method of choice on a card or two to figure out if it will turn out as expected.

GENERAL INFORMATION

Before picking one of the methods below, make two decisions:

1. The purpose of the blessing.
    Do you want to increase sales, expand your network or gain new clients? Whatever you decide will dictate the colours and ingredients you use.
2. Whether you want the blessing to be visible/detectable by the recipients of the cards/advertisements.
    This will depend on the purpose of the blessing and the industry you are in. If you are a spiritual coach, a witch for hire or tarot reader, you may not care if your business cards smell like juniper and lemon. However, if your career isn't as friendly to esoteric practices, you'll want to do things that fly under the radar.

TIMING

Plan your work during the waxing moon. Perform the blessing on the full moon.

Method 1: Incense

This technique is the most subtle of all. You can charm your advertising materials or business cards without leaving a trace. After you pick the purpose of your spell and choose an incense that supports your intent (*see* "A Garden of Abundance" on page 156 for information about herbal incense ingredients), follow these steps.

SUPPLIES

- Incense
- An incense holder
- Business cards

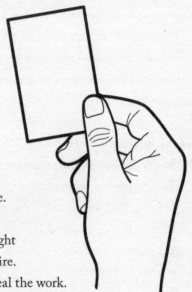

STEPS

1. Put the incense in a sturdy holder and light it.
2. Take a stack of business cards and pass it through the incense smoke. As you do, picture your cards going out into the world, getting into the right hands and bringing you what you desire.
3. Incorporate a statement of intent to seal the work.
4. After you have finished, you can put your cards directly into your wallet or card holder – they are ready to go!

Method 2: Fancy edges

This technique is visible but fairly subtle. You can probably get away with it in all but the strictest corporate environments.

SUPPLIES

- A broad-tipped marker of the appropriate colour
- Your business cards

STEPS

1. Pick the purpose of your spell. For example, you might want your business cards to help you network more successfully, draw attention or bring new paying customers.

2. Using the colours in "The Colours of Wealth" on page 143, pick one that corresponds to your intent. For example, you might choose grey (overcome obstacles, know what to say) to help you network, red (power, ambition) or pink (attract others, success) to draw attention to you or your business, or green (money, prosperity) to bring paying customers.

3. Tightly hold a stack of your business cards and colour in the edges with the colour corresponding to your intent. As you do, picture your cards going out into the world, getting into the right hands and bringing you what you desire.

4. Incorporate a statement of intent to seal the work. Examples:
   - "Grow my network, sound and sure."
   - "Bring me attention and interest."
   - "Paying customers, come to me."

5. Put your business cards on your wealth altar or in another safe place to allow the edges to dry.

Note:

Some printers offer coloured edges for business cards and other products, so you can order them pre-printed with the colour of your choice. If you do, follow the instructions above without using a marker. Just use the pointer finger of the hand you write with to rub the edges of the card while you visualize and state your intent.

Method 3: Herbs and oils and stones

This technique varies in its subtlety, based on the types of oils and herbs you choose and how long you decide to infuse them with their influences. If you follow these steps, you might end up with business cards that smell like flowers or incense, which can be wonderful if it suits your industry! As with the other methods, select your purpose, and then choose herbs or essential oils to support it. (*See* "A Garden of Abundance" on page 156.)

SUPPLIES

- Herbs, stones, essential oils and/or magical oils
- Gauze bags (if using herbs)
- Cotton balls, discs or tissues
- A large airtight container you can seal tightly
- Personal prosperity sigil (optional)

STEPS

1. If you are using herbs, start with them. Put a generous pinch or piece of each herb in the gauze bag. For each herb, visualize the influence it will have on your cards and state what you want it to do.
    Example: "Oregano, bring me money", while
    picturing money flooding your way.
2. Put the gauze bag in the airtight container.
3. If you are using oils, put a dab of each oil on a cotton pad. As you do, visualize the influence it will have on your cards and state what you want it to do.
    Example: "Attraction oil, draw people's interest", while picturing people reacting to your card by reaching out to contact you.
4. Put the cotton pad(s) in the container.
5. Place a stack of business cards on the other side of the container.
6. If you are using your personal prosperity sigil, place a
    drawing of it on top of your stack of cards. Say, "I seal this
    work with the mark of my perpetual prosperity."

7. Close the container while saying, "Components all, come together to bless my cards so that [state your intent]."
8. Put the container on your wealth altar or in another safe place.
9. Let the cards remain with the herbs and/or oils for at least 24 hours.

> **Note:** When you take the cards out of the container, give them a sniff test. Depending on the herbs and oils you used, the cards may have absorbed their scent. No matter how delightful the scent, you might not want your cards to smell herbal. If so, air the cards out for a day or two and the scent should fade away.

HUNTING FOR TREASURE

As discussed in the opening chapters of this book, everyone has different definitions of prosperity and wealth. The concept of wealth extends beyond money, encompassing things like material possessions, security and time. The same thing goes for treasure – it can mean many things to many people. Physical wealth, the freedom to travel or the time to indulge in your hobbies all might seem like treasure to you. When I want to find something I'll treasure (whether I know what I want it to be or not), I use the talisman below to lead my steps in the right direction.

TIMING
Any time you want to hunt for treasure!

SUPPLIES
- A black fine-point marker
- A pencil
- An eraser
- Paper (approximately 10x10cm [4"x4"])

STEPS

1. Using a pencil, lightly sketch the design below on the piece of paper. Try to make it as accurate as possible, but it doesn't have to be perfect.

2. Make sure you can complete this next part from start to finish without stopping or getting up. Use the black marker to draw over the talisman's design, making a final permanent copy.

3. When you are finished drawing the talisman, write some information that identifies you on the paper. It could be your name, magical name, date of birth or astrological signs.

4. Fold the paper into quarters and hold it between your palms. Say, "Lead my feet to treasure most sweet. Show me the way to what I crave." Close your eyes and see yourself discovering treasure. You can make this visualization specific to a particular item (the perfect latte, a book you've been looking for, a reasonably priced used car) or you can see yourself delighting in something unexpected.

5. Put the talisman in your right shoe. If possible, put it under the lining of your shoe to hold it in place and keep it from quickly wearing out. Keep it in your shoe until you find your treasure.

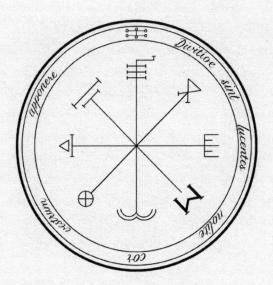

INCREASE YOUR WEALTH WITH A MANIFESTATION BOWL

When you create a manifestation bowl, you are engaging in a spiritual and magical practice that helps you focus your intent and shape your future so that you can manifest your deepest wishes. Manifestation bowls are constructed from many different components which are each associated with your desired outcome. They are an excellent method to turn to if you don't have enough room for a full-sized wealth altar. Once you create a manifestation bowl, you will work with it repeatedly over time so that you can continue to contribute energy and intention to it. They are constructed in many ways. They don't even need to incorporate a bowl and they don't need to reside in a special location! No matter their shape or construction, all manifestation bowls share a few attributes.

- Manifestation bowls are intentional. To create one, a goal or purpose is selected. This goal or theme will influence the decisions that are made when constructing the bowl.
- Manifestation bowls are assembled in either a container or demarcated space, where selected items with magical significance are arranged in such a way as to both symbolize the intent of the bowl and magically enhance the influences of the components used to make the bowl.
- Manifestation bowls are tended to and worked with over time. After the initial construction of the bowl, you will regularly return to the bowl to contribute more magical components, imagery and intent.
- While you can create a manifestation bowl for any purpose (love, focus, friendship), we will focus on how to create one for drawing you toward a future of prosperous wealth.

TIMING

Create your manifestation bowl on a Sunday when the sun is shining brightly. Or you can choose to make your bowl on the night of a full moon.

LOCATION

A manifestation bowl makes a great centrepiece on a wealth or household altar. If you don't have an altar, a quiet corner in your kitchen or living room will work just as well.

If you want to make a manifestation bowl for your place of business, decide if you want it to be public, semi-private or completely private. You can locate your prosperity manifestation bowl near your business entrance, behind the counter or in a backroom, depending on how open you want to be with it. If you make your bowl a public one, don't be surprised if your guests ask questions or even want to interact with it!

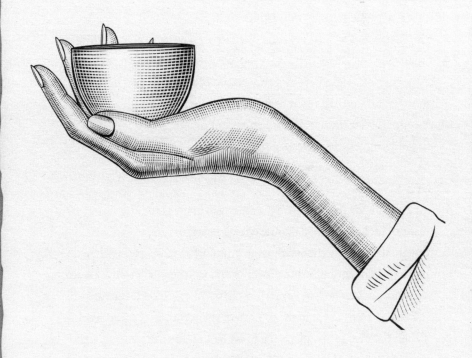

SUPPLIES

> **Note:**
> You can customize your bowl based on any specific goal you might want to include with your general prosperity work by selecting herbs, crystals/stones, and other items specific to your individual desires. The components in the supply list below are suggestions, but you can select the items that make the most sense to you.

- A container. I usually use a silver pedestal bowl. However, you can select whatever appeals to you and your aesthetic. It will be helpful if you select something that speaks of wealth or prosperity to you.
- A base substance. It should be some kind of small item that represents plenty. Think dried rice, beans or grains. I have a bag of tiny tumbled stones that I like to use.
- Prosperity and wealth herbs like whole bay leaves, a whole nutmeg and rosemary
- Prosperity and wealth crystals like citrine, pyrite and malachite
- Small symbols of wealth like a few small-denomination coins, a drawing of a dollar sign, a tiny statue of a wealth god or goddess, or anything that represents prosperity to you
- A copy of your personal prosperity sigil drawn on gold or green paper (optional)

STEPS

1. At the time of your choosing, gather the items you want to include in your manifestation bowl.
2. Spiritually cleanse the bowl, stones and other items you will be using by passing them through some incense smoke or using another cleansing method. As you do, say something like, "Clear and cleanse any disruptive influences from these items to perfect them for my magical work."
3. When you feel ready, place the bowl or container on your work surface and say, "With this bowl I create my future. It manifests perpetual prosperity."

4. If you are using your personal prosperity sigil, place it face up in the centre of the bottom of the bowl. Say, "My sign of perpetual prosperity fuels my work."

5. Pick up the base substance and say, "This is the fertile ground in which I plant my seeds. This is the foundation for my dreams, let my structure be sound." Then pour the base substance into the bowl. Depending on the type of material you use, you may wish to work with it before moving on to the next step. For example, you may wish to spread it out more evenly across the bottom of your container, create small mounds with it if you don't want to work on a flat surface, or draw patterns in it. For prosperity manifestation, I like to draw rays from the centre to the edges of the bowl. After the base substance/your foundation is arranged to your liking, move on to the next step.

6. Now it is time to arrange all the items that symbolize wealth and prosperity in your manifestation bowl. For each item, hold it and state why you are including it and what your intent is. For example, you could place a small citrine in the bowl and say, "I add this citrine so that it blesses me with active wealth-building and clarity of thought." Arranging these items may take some time, even if you previously experimented with how to arrange them. Take it slow and enjoy the creative process. Feel the energy in each item and the collective energy of the bowl and make your decisions intuitively based on what you are building.

7. If you wish to include any powdered herbs, sprinkling powders or perfumes, add them after you are finished arranging the larger components. Use the same procedure as you did for all the other items. Hold the item, and describe what you are doing and what your intent is.

8. After you finish constructing the bowl, take a few moments to admire it and to sense its power. If you want to make any adjustments, make them before the next step. (You can make changes to your manifestation bowl as long as it exists, but it is good to start out being as satisfied as possible with the arrangement.)

9. When you feel ready, prepare to activate your manifestation bowl and put it to work. You can do this in several ways.

THE GOLDEN GRIMOIRE

Whichever way you choose, make sure you have a clear image of what you want to manifest in your mind.

- If you placed your personal prosperity sigil under the base substance of your manifestation bowl, you can activate it by tracing the sigil over the bowl while saying, "Work for me now. Draw prosperity and wealth to me at all times."
- If you want to work with a god, goddess or other entity, you can pray for them to bless your bowl and activate it for you.
- If you want to summon energy from the earth, you can place your hands over the bowl and visualize drawing it up through your feet and channelling it down your arms and out your hands, charging the bowl with energy and your desires.

10. Tend your manifestation bowl on a regular basis (daily, weekly, monthly). This may include spending some time with it and praying or otherwise giving energy to it. Or you could speak your intention out loud while you add a pinch of a powdered herb to the bowl. You could also place a candle near the bowl and burn it for a short time every day. Regular interaction with the bowl keeps it working for you and reinforces your goals.

You can keep your altar bowl for as long as you choose. I usually keep mine going until I reach my magical goal. As this bowl is meant to keep you in a state of constant prosperity, you can make it a permanent fixture on your wealth altar. However, don't feel as though you must keep it around forever. You can deconstruct the bowl at any time. Just remember that it will take some time to get up to its full strength.

When I want to deconstruct a manifestation bowl, I thank it for all it has done for me. Then I carefully take it apart. I physically and spiritually cleanse the items I want to keep, and I dispose of the rest by wrapping them in white paper and throwing them away. Once I clean my bowl, I am ready to pick a new intention and create the next one!

DOWSING TO FIND THE RIGHT HELP

At some point, you might be faced with the need to find the right kind of expert to help you on your financial journey. Whether you are simply seeking out someone who has been through what you are experiencing (working your way out of debt, starting your own online store, changing careers) or looking for a professional such as an accountant, tax preparer or attorney, it can be a challenge to find someone that is not only trustworthy and knowledgeable but who you also click with.

This spell will help you identify reliable folks who can help you. As in all things, don't just go off the magical information you receive from this spell. Interview people, ask questions and get an understanding of their personalities before deciding who to trust. It is a good rule of thumb that if the person helping you isn't happy when you are asking questions, they aren't the person to work with.

TIMING
As this is a divination method, you can do it at any time. If you feel as though your intuitive powers are stronger during the full moon, do it during that moon phase.

SUPPLIES
- A pendulum (you can use an actual pendulum or any long string with a weight on the end)
- Representations of the people who might be able to help you
- A table

STEPS

1. Take some time to get familiar with your divination tool. Find a comfortable way to hold the pendulum's chain. If your pendulum is made of crystal or metal, hold it in your hands to warm it. You might feel moved to spiritually cleanse the pendulum before you use it. If so, use something appropriate for whatever your pendulum is made of. You can use incense smoke, salt or blessed water to clean it.

2. Calm your mind. Let the pendulum dangle from your hand. Take some deep breaths.

3. When you feel ready, ask the pendulum to show you how it will move when it is indicating someone who will help you and you will get along with. Note how it moves.

4. Next ask the pendulum to show you how it will move when it is indicating someone who won't be helpful or who you won't get along with. Note how it moves.

5. Then ask the pendulum to show you how it will move when it is indicating someone who will be middle-of-the-road (neither great nor terrible to work with). Note how it moves. This step is optional. I find it useful. If it makes things too confusing, you can skip it.

6. Spread out representations of the people you are trying to decide between on the table. Make sure they are far enough apart so you can use the pendulum to consider each one individually. You can use many different things to represent potential helpers:
   - Business cards
   - Names or business names written on small pieces of paper
   - A map with places marked on it

7. Brace your elbow on the table and let the pendulum dangle over the representation of the first person or business. Ask the pendulum something like, "How would working with this person to [insert activity] be?"

8. Breathe steadily and be patient. Watch for the pendulum to move. You may get a definite response right away or you might need to wait a while. Don't get frustrated or annoyed if you need to wait. Dowsing with a pendulum is a delicate art, but it's worth learning.

9. Once you get a response for the first person or business, move on to the next one and repeat steps 7–8.

10. Note the people who will be good helpers.

If you end up with more than one good candidate, ask the pendulum to show you how it will move when it is over the best candidate. Then hold the pendulum over each one and wait for a response.

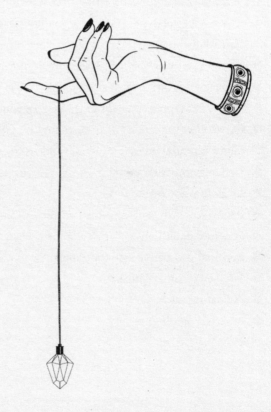

FOUR-ELEMENT HOUSEHOLD WEALTH OLIVE OIL LAMP

This is a magical way to maintain and sustain a state of wealth. Once your household is stable and settled, and you wish to preserve your achievements, build this lamp and burn it for an hour at least once a week. This method requires a floating wick, which you can find online or at candle supply companies. The beauty of this simple yet powerful magical tool will bless your household and fuel your efforts to maintain and grow your wealth.

TIMING
On a Sunday during a full moon.

SUPPLIES
- Salt
- Water
- A glass jar (approximately 13cm [5"] high and 8cm [3"] across)
- Olive oil
- Clove essential oil
- Lemongrass essential oil
- Frankincense essential oil
- Paper
- A pen or pencil
- Personal prosperity sigil (optional)
- Food colouring (optional)
- A floating wick
- Matches or a lighter

STEPS

1. Fill the jar halfway with water. Say, "Blessed water of life, help us to flow with whatever life brings us so that we are continuously surrounded by wealth and joy."

2. Add a few drops of food colouring if you want coloured water. I use green, but you can use any colour suited to your situation (*see* "The Colours of Wealth" on page 143).
Note: If you use water-based food colouring, the olive oil will not change colour.

3. Put three pinches of salt in the water. Say, "Creature of earth, ground our efforts. Make them manifest in physical reality."

4. Fill the jar the rest of the way with olive oil until it is a few centimetres (one or two inches) below the rim of the jar. Say, "Fuel for the fire, be the engine of this work so that it is perpetually sustained."

5. Give the oil and water time to separate.

6. Add three drops of clove essential oil to the jar. Say, "Clove oil, bless my house with your scent. Make space and make way so that wealth can remain. Drive out disruption."

7. Add five drops of lemongrass essential oil to the jar. Say, "Lemongrass oil, bless my house with your scent. Keep our energy elevated, bring us bright ideas and creative solutions to our problems and for our plans."

8. Add nine drops of frankincense essential oil to the jar. Say, "Frankincense, bless my house with your scent. Fill all who dwell in it with the wisdom and commitment to positive and constructive actions that will benefit the house and maintain our wealth."

9. Place the floating wick in the jar so it floats on top of the oil.

10. Write out your intention on a piece of paper. You can write it out in words or you can draw your personal prosperity sigil. You might write something like "This house is in a state of perpetual wealth."

11. Fold the paper and place it under the jar.

12. Light the lamp.

13. Meditate for at least five minutes while the lamp burns. During this time, you can either visualize your intention (your house remaining prosperous and happy) or you can allow your mind to drift so you can receive intuitive messages.

14. You can leave the lamp burning on your wealth altar or in another safe place. Don't leave it unattended. After it has burned for about an hour, extinguish it.

Burn the lamp for an hour at least once a week. Replenish the olive oil and essential oils when necessary. When you replenish the essential oils, repeat statements similar to the ones provided in steps 6–8.

RULER OF THE HOUSE

From time to time, my household's atmosphere starts to feel stagnant or unsettled. Little things start going wrong. Appointments get delayed. Maybe my sales or bookings slow down. The general luck of the household takes a downturn. It usually affects the entire family and can cause some serious problems for all the money-earners in the house. If you experience something similar, this simple sweet spell can drive out all disruptions and get things back on track. It will welcome in positive energy, bring good luck and elevate everyone's spirits. It puts you in control and allows you to get things back on track.

I don't usually perform this spell at my wealth altar. Instead, I choose a central place in my home so I can ensure the influence of the candles and incense spread throughout the house.

TIMING
Any time things around your home don't feel quite right.

SUPPLIES
- Rose incense
- Dragon's blood incense
- A purple candle, any size (if you work with a larger candle, you can use it several times)
- A candleholder
- An incense holder
- A toothpick or other carving tool

STEPS

1. Find a quiet place to work. I like to use my kitchen or dining room table.
2. Carve the word "LUCK" on either side of the candle.
3. Hold the candle in your hand and tell it what you want it to do. Say something like, "Cleanse the energy of this house, remove any obstacles from our paths, and bless all who live here."
4. Put the candle in the candleholder.
5. Choose a place to burn the candle. Make sure it's a safe place where it won't get knocked down or run into.
6. Light the candle and the incense. Say, "May the light from this candle drive out any and all disruptive influences."
7. Allow the incense to burn out. Let the candle burn for at least an hour.

TO QUICKLY RENT A ROOM OR PROPERTY (TO THE RIGHT PERSON)

I've never dabbled in real estate, so I've never had to go through the process of renting out a room or property. However, I have had to find a roommate right away, which can become stressful when rent is coming due and you don't know who's going to pay for half! This spell will help in either situation. It draws a renter/roommate who you will get along with and who will be reliable when it comes to paying their bills.

TIMING

Any time you want to rent a room/property or get a roommate.

SUPPLIES

- A white bowl
- A white candle
- A candleholder
- Water
- Salt
- Bergamot oil
- Bergamot petals or white rose petals (optional)

STEPS

1. Place the white bowl in the centre of the place you want to rent.
2. Hold the candle in the hand you write with and tell it what you want.
    Be specific.
    Example: "Bring me a tenant who is trustworthy, pays
    their rent on time and will respect my property."

3. Put the candle in its holder and place it in the centre of the bowl.

4. Pour in enough water to cover the bottom third of the candle.

5. Put your hand in the water. Say, "Peaceful water, bring calm and tranquillity to this property. Draw a tenant/roommate who will appreciate the atmosphere."

6. Put four generous pinches of salt in the bowl, one in each of the four cardinal directions. Say, "Sacred salt, whether they come from north, south, east or west, bring me a tenant/roommate that's the best."

7. Put 13 drops of bergamot oil in the water. Say, "Crisp citrus, energize this place and make it attractive, cosy and welcoming for the perfect tenant/roommate."

8. Stir the water in the bowl.

9. Float the bergamot petals or rose petals in the bowl (if you are using them).

10. Light the candle. Say, "Constant beacon, cast a spiritual light and bring me the perfect tenant/roommate."

11. Let the candle burn for at least 30 minutes. Don't leave the candle unattended while it burns. During this time, dip your hand in the floral water you've created and sprinkle some in each corner of the room or rental property. You can also sprinkle it on the windowsills. While you do, picture enjoying easy and happy relations between yourself and your future tenant/roommate.

FLAMES OF WEALTH: A 31-DAY SPELL FOR GROWTH AND GAIN

Two of my favourite sayings about wealth are *"Il denaro è il fratello del denaro"* ("Money is the brother of money") and *"Il guadagno fa guadagno"* ("Gain makes gain"). Both of these proverbs remind us that like attracts like. Keeping that in mind, this spell isn't for times when you are in dire need of cash. It should only be used after you have established a solid financial foundation. The purpose of this spell is to expand and build upon your current financial situation. It can be used to draw more wealth to you personally or to your business.

This magical act combines the key concepts of attention, gratitude, effort and constancy. Your repeated actions while performing the work will establish a magical pattern that grows more powerful every day. The growth continues after the 31st day, so expect to continue to reap the benefits of this working.

NOTES

🔥 This spell takes time and a large number of supplies, including 31 green candles and 469 coins or paper bills.

🔥 It is best to do each day's work at the same time every day. However, you can vary the time if necessary.

🔥 If you miss a day, start over the following month. This spell depends on momentum and building a pattern.

🔥 I have documented the spell as if it is being worked in a month that has 31 days, but you can begin this spell on the first of any month. Just keep in mind that in a 28-, 29- or 30-day month, you won't be performing the daily work as many times.

SUPPLIES

- 31 small green candles (or fewer, depending on how many days in the month there are)
- A candleholder that will fit one candle at a time
- A bowl or platter large enough to hold all the money (I like to use a silver-coloured one)
- Your personal prosperity sigil drawn with green ink on white paper (optional, but strongly recommended)
- 496 coins or paper bills (I use pennies or dollars)
- A polishing cloth or other method to shine a coin (if you are using coins)
- A workspace where you can leave your work undisturbed throughout the entire month
- An image, statue or representation of an entity with whom you wish to work (an ancestor, a god or goddess you often work with, or a god or goddess that rules prosperity and wealth would all be good choices)

Day 1

THIS DAY'S GOALS

- Set up the magical workspace that you will use throughout the month. Be sure to select a place that will remain undisturbed throughout the month. Try to choose a place that is easily accessible. A location like a quiet corner of your desk or a low shelf or bookcase would be excellent. If you have an altar, that would be the perfect location.
- Perform the first day's work.

SUPPLIES FOR THIS DAY

- The bowl or platter
- One green candle
- The candleholder
- One coin or piece of paper money
- A polishing cloth or other method to shine a coin (if you are using coins)
- The representation of the entity you will be working with

STEPS

1. Gather your supplies.
2. Prepare your magical workspace.
3. Prepare yourself.
4. Place your personal prosperity sigil face up in the centre of your workspace. Put the palm of the hand you write with on top of the sigil. Say, "By this sign I extend the influence of personal prosperity throughout this work." You can also address the entity you are working with to request their ongoing assistance.
5. Position the bowl or platter in the centre of your workspace on top of the sigil.
6. Place the representation of the entity at the back of the altar.
7. Place the candle between the image of the entity and the bowl. Make sure you use a sturdy candleholder that fits the candle well.
8. Place your collected money close by but not on the altar. A nearby drawer or shelf works well.
9. Light the candle and say, "And so I start. This work will grow my wealth. Its influence will continue after the work is done."
10. As the candle burns, select one of the coins or paper bills you have collected.
    - If you are working with a coin, carefully polish and shine the coin.
    - If you are working with a paper bill, carefully fold it lengthwise toward yourself twice.

11. While you are preparing the money, picture yourself
    prosperous and wealthy while saying:
    > *Draw round, draw round*
    > *All wealth to be found,*
    > *Grow and gain, gain and grow,*
    > *To me wealth will flow.*

12. Toss the piece of money into the bowl. (It's nice if you are
    using a coin because it will make a satisfying clink.)

13. State one thing you are grateful for about your current financial situation.
    Follow it with a statement of intent about your future.
    Example: "I am so thankful that I don't have to live paycheque to
    paycheque any more. I will save $5,000 by the end of the year."
    Try to make a different statement of gratitude every day.
    You can keep the same statement of intent, or you can change
    it according to your preferences and financial goals.

14. Seal the spell by drawing your personal prosperity
    sigil in the air over the bowl.

15. Say a prayer to your helping entity or request their help/blessings. Listen
    for any messages or hints from the entity or the universe at large.

16. Allow the green candle to burn as long as you can. It's preferable
    to let it burn out, but you can extinguish it if you need to.

Days 2–30

EACH DAY'S GOALS

- Count and prepare the amount of money to contribute to your spell bowl.
- Deposit the money into the bowl.
- Make your combined statement of gratitude and intent.
- Pray/talk to the entity you are working with.
- Listen for important messages or guidance.

SUPPLIES FOR EACH DAY

🔥 One green candle

🔥 One more coin or piece of paper money than you worked with the day before.

For example: on day 2 you will work with two pieces, on day 3 you will work with three pieces, on day 4 you will work with four pieces, etc.

🔥 A polishing cloth or other method to shine a coin (if you are using coins)

STEPS

1. Gather your supplies.
2. Prepare yourself.
3. Replace the old candle stub with a new candle. Light the new candle.
4. As the candle burns, select the appropriate number of coins or paper bills you have collected.
   - 🔥 If you are working with a coin, carefully polish and shine the coin.
   - 🔥 If you are working with a paper bill, carefully fold it lengthwise toward yourself twice.
5. While you are preparing the money, picture yourself prosperous and wealthy while saying:

   Draw round, draw round
   All wealth to be found,
   Grow and gain, gain and grow,
   To me wealth will flow.

6. As you finish preparing each piece of money, toss it into the bowl.
7. State one thing you are grateful for about your current financial situation. Follow it with a statement of intent about your future.
   Example: "I am so thankful that I don't have to live paycheque to paycheque any more. I will save $5,000 by the end of the year."
   Try to make a different statement of gratitude every day.
   You can keep the same statement of intent, or you can change it according to your preferences and financial goals.
8. Seal the spell by drawing your personal prosperity sigil in the air over the bowl.

THE GOLDEN GRIMOIRE

9. Say a prayer to your helping entity or request their help/blessings. Listen for any messages or hints from the entity or the universe at large.
10. Allow the green candle to burn as long as you can. It's preferable to let it burn out, but you can extinguish it if you need to.

Day 31

THIS DAY'S GOAL
🔥 Perform the last day's work

SUPPLIES FOR THIS DAY
🔥 One green candle
🔥 31 coins or pieces of paper money
🔥 A polishing cloth or other method to shine a coin (if you are using coins)

STEPS
1. Gather your supplies.
2. Prepare yourself.
3. Replace the old candle stub with a new candle. Light the new candle.
4. As the candle burns, select the appropriate number of coins or paper bills you have collected.
    🔥 If you are working with a coin, carefully polish and shine the coin.
    🔥 If you are working with a paper bill, carefully fold it lengthwise toward yourself twice.
5. While you are preparing the money, picture yourself prosperous and wealthy while saying:

    Draw round, draw round
    All wealth to be found,
    Grow and gain, gain and grow,
    To me wealth will flow.

6. As you finish preparing each piece of money, toss it into the bowl.

7. State one thing you are grateful for about your current financial situation.
    Follow it with a statement of intent about your future.
    Example: "I am so thankful that I don't have to live paycheque to
    paycheque any more. I will save $5,000 by the end of the year."
    Try to make a different statement of gratitude every day.
    You can keep the same statement of intent, or you can change
    it according to your preferences and financial goals.

8. Seal the spell by drawing your personal prosperity
    sigil in the air over the bowl.

9. Say a prayer to your helping entity or request their help/blessings. Listen
    for any messages or hints from the entity or the universe at large.

10. Allow the green candle to burn as long as you
    can. It's preferable to let it burn out, but
    you can extinguish it if you need to.

11. When the green candle is finished
    burning, return to your workspace
    and say, "And so this work is finished
    but there is no end to my prosperous
    wealth. My money draws money,
    I prosper, my wealth grows."

FINISHING YOUR WORK

Dispose of any remnants of candle wax appropriately by wrapping them in white paper and placing them in the trash (it's not good for the environment to dispose of wax remnants outside).

I like to finish this spell by speaking a general blessing over the money I used and then putting it back out into circulation to bless other people's finances.

For example, I'll place my hands palm down over the bowl of money and say, "May this money bring money to anyone who finds it, spends it or saves it. May it draw cash to those in need and help build the wealth of anyone who comes into contact with it."

If I am working with paper money, I will either spend it over time or bring it to a bank to convert it into larger denominations, which will allow for the blessed bills to get into circulation more quickly. If I am working with pennies, I might do the same, but I also reserve some to "accidentally" drop on the ground in highly trafficked areas for people to find. There's nothing like finding an extra-lucky penny! You may also wish to give some of the cash to friends or family to bless them.

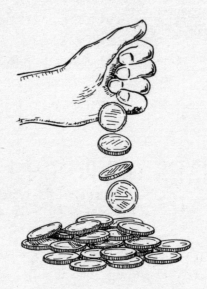

GROUP WORK

Once upon a time, working with a group meant everyone had to gather in one place at the same time and contribute their energy in the same way. Unless you were lucky enough to know a group of people who were comfortable with spell work, it meant finding and joining an organization like a coven. This often included adhering to a code or system of beliefs that the coven promoted. In my younger days, I attended many pagan meet-and-greets and other social events, searching for people who had practices similar to mine. I met a lot of amazing friends that way, and was able to join and form covens and other magical organizations in the process. This approach is still viable if you live in a part of the world that supports a community of magically minded folks, and I highly recommend it.

However, these days, there are new approaches that offer us a greater variety of experiences, even if we live in places where there aren't a lot of folks interested in exploring the world of magic. This section will cover what to consider if you want to convert the spells in this book into group workings. We'll also take a look at all the different ways we can use modern communication methods to connect with others and work magic.

It is important to remember that with all group work, you make yourself vulnerable to others both emotionally and spiritually. So don't force yourself to work with someone who doesn't feel right to you. Even if they don't mean you harm, your discomfort is likely to inhibit your ability to contribute energy to the work.

WHAT'S THE POINT OF GROUP WORK?

Depending on your personality, the idea of group work might be endlessly intriguing or completely off-putting. As with all aspects of magic, there is no single correct way, even when it comes to including others in your spiritual work. If you don't like the idea, you don't even have to consider it. But here are the benefits of finding other folks to work with.

- Despite our best efforts, magical work can be complex and confusing at times, especially when starting out. Having a friend or two to bounce ideas off or brainstorm with can help you figure out what you want and what magical techniques you should use to get it. Sometimes just talking about an issue with someone else is all you need to allay your fears and answer your own questions.
- Interacting with other magic users, even ones that are just starting out, can help introduce you to ideas and techniques that you may not consider otherwise.
- When more than one person contributes energy toward a magical intention, the effectiveness of that energy seems to multiply. Joint efforts usually become more than just the sum of their parts.
- When it is difficult for you to focus on your intention (for example, if you are sick and want to do healing work), a friend can help by doing the work for you. This can be particularly useful with wealth magic. Your friend might be able to summon up the conviction that you deserve a financially sound life before you can. You can each support the other until you reach a point where your wealth wounds heal enough to allow you to work on your own behalf.
- The power of the other. There is something particularly magical in allowing someone else to do work for you. There are times when someone else's smallest effort can be more effective than all your previous attempts. I don't mean that we are weaker when working on our own or for ourselves. I think this is just the universe's reminder that we should all work together to bless each other.

TYPES OF GROUP WORK

- Working in unison (in person) – This is usually what first springs to mind when we discuss doing magical work in a group setting. Gather at the appointed place and time and make a coordinated magical effort. This is a beautiful way to experience magic, though you might find yourself needing to get over some magical stage fright when it is your turn to speak or perform part of the spell or ritual. This isn't uncommon and it still happens to me from time to time, especially if I get out of the habit.

- Working in unison (remotely) – I've had great success working with small groups over video chat. This approach takes a little bit more preparation on everyone's part because if any magical materials or tools are involved, everyone needs to make the effort to get them ready before the appointed time. However, there is a lot that can be done with everyone using a single white candle (they don't all have to match) or another common tool. Or you can experiment with someone officiating the spell and manipulating a single set of tools while the other participants contribute energy to the work. The most difficult part of this approach for me is making sure I have enough space on my desk to use it as an altar. (Yes, my desk is always cluttered!)

- Reciprocal work – If you have a friend or two that enjoys working magic as much as you do, this is a fun way to participate in a group working. Reciprocal work is simply each practitioner working on behalf of the other. You can approach this kind of work in one of two ways.

  1. Pick matching topics and methods (for example, improving your careers by creating a herbal bag). In this case, each person would create and charge or bless a bag for the other person.

  2. Pick different topics and methods (one person may pick finding the perfect location for her new business, while the other might pick keeping their well-paying job). In this case, each person would choose the technique they are most comfortable with and then do the work on behalf of the other. This method

usually takes some conversation and negotiation so each person understands what the other will be doing on their behalf.

- Working on someone's behalf – Unlike reciprocal work above, this is just doing work for another magically minded person when they need it. This could include burning a candle for success when they are at a job interview, or any other kind of magic. If you have some close friends who practise magic, you can build a mutual support network where you step in to help each other when needed.

- Ceremonial magic – This is the most complex variety of group work. This approach requires all participants to agree on a mutual goal. Then a ceremony is designed to harness magical power and direct it to that specific intent. Each person must learn the part they must play in the ceremony. Depending on how formal you want to get with the proceedings, this can be a resource-intensive method, requiring a lot of supplies. Of course, if you are working with a group, everyone can contribute materials, including ceremony planning.

- Item construction – There's nothing quite so fun as sitting around and making a magical tool with a group of friends. Whether you are doing something as simple as brewing up a magical tea or colouring tarot cards, or diving into something more complex like making the Money-Drawing Shaker Box on page 200, you can have a wonderful time including others in the process. Experiment with each person contributing to a single item. Or you can have everyone make their own version and then pile them up to receive a group blessing from everyone involved.

- Concepts and power-building – Though not necessarily a conscious part of group work, this is one of its benefits. This result is often so subtle that people don't recognize it, so I want to make sure to call attention to it. When you work with a group, certain concepts, tools and ideas start to take on a greater significance, and through that process, they grow in strength for the members of the group. Repeated use of the same item or idea empowers it and makes it more effective. Here are a couple of examples:

1. Decades ago, I was in a coven, and we used light-blue candles

THE GOLDEN GRIMOIRE

for all our healing work. To this day, that's the first colour I turn to when I do magical work for healing. That colour has become the *sine qua non* for all my healing magic.

2. While writing this book, I discussed the topic of wealth magic with Black Candle Coven, a group of people who meet every Wednesday night to discuss magical concepts and support each other's spiritual and magical journeys. Recently, we were discussing the types of money magic everyone used (I *may* have been responsible for bringing up the subject, considering I was working on this book at the time). At one point, I asked everyone to share their favourite money magic spells with the group. Plenty of wonderful ideas were shared. Hollis suggested burning a style of incense called "Attracts Money". She reported that she experienced great success every time she burned it – so much so that she didn't burn it too often because it made her feel greedy! Burning the incense resulted in her receiving money unexpectedly and legal matters being resolved in her family's favour. Members of the coven have purchased the same incense and have had some successes. As each success story is shared, the power of the incense is reinforced for the members of the group. Now "Attracts Money" incense is a key part of my magical practice!

THE GOLDEN GRIMOIRE

ADAPTING SPELLS FOR GROUP WORK

All the spells in this book can be adapted for two or more people. Some lend themselves more easily to adaptation. For example, the Wealth Wound Cleansing Bath on page 52 isn't the easiest to adapt to group work unless you have intimate partners to work your magic with. Also, particularly when working magic to deal with bad habits, it might be difficult to open up and be fully vulnerable in a group setting, so choose carefully.

Here are some tips for selecting and adapting spells for group work.

1. In general, the fewer supplies and components a spell uses, the easier it is to adapt for groups who don't share a household. If people need to gather their own supplies or tools, keep the materials list to a minimum to make it easier for everyone.

2. When doing group work, prepare to be flexible. Unless one person is going to supply all the materials, accept the fact that not everyone will have matching candleholders. Or someone may only have a white candle and not the colour specified in the spell (remember that white candles can be used for anything). Some of the participants may not have access to fresh herbs and so they could show up with dried versions. Reserve some time before starting to see what's on hand and make any necessary adjustments.

3. If you are the one in charge of coordinating a group working, communication is key. If you feel like you are overcommunicating, you are probably doing it right! Realize that even when someone has questions, they may not be willing to voice them, for fear of appearing uninformed or unskilled. So be sure to anticipate questions others may have and answer them clearly. Explain the steps of the spell before you start. Explain them as you go. If you are coordinating the working, you are acting as a guide helping to see everyone through the experience.

4. If the work requires any preparation before the group working,

remind people regularly to ensure they complete it before the day of the working. Also, decide beforehand what will happen if someone hasn't done the prework. Are the steps something they can do before the working starts? (If so, see item 2 about remaining flexible, and reserve some time beforehand to adjust.) Will they be able to participate anyway? Will they have to wait until next time? Make sure everyone understands this up front to avoid hurt feelings.

5. Consider how specific you need the timing of the spell to be. If you want to start working the spell right when the moon becomes full, you have to make sure everyone shows up on time. That means giving a start time that will allow sufficient leeway for stragglers to arrive and get ready. To make things easier, if you aren't used to working with all involved, choose a timing method that allows you a lot of flexibility, like a day of the week or general phase of the moon.

6. If you are coordinating the working, practise the steps on your own. You'll likely be a little bit nervous if you aren't used to leading people through a process. You will be much more confident if you have practised the physical components of the spell before it's time to work them for real. Even if you aren't the one leading the work, it may be a good idea to practise so you feel less nervous and can more easily focus on your intentions.

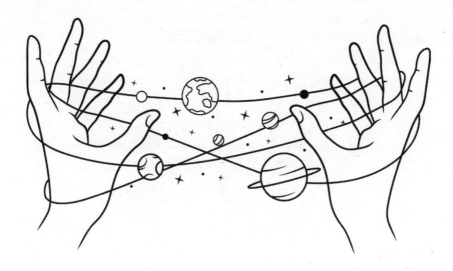

THE GOLDEN GRIMOIRE

THE QUESTION OF COMMUNAL SUPPLIES

If you find yourself working in person with the same partner or group of people repeatedly, consider storing a communal set of supplies and commonly used materials. Have a discussion with your group members and talk through the topics below.

1. Decide where the materials will be stored. Try to keep them at the place where you meet most often. If the place regularly changes, the person who participates most often will be the best person to store them, if they have space.

2. Figure out how the materials will be purchased. Will everyone make a one-time contribution or regular contributions?

3. Decide how much if any of the supplies should be available to members of the group for individual use.

4. Decide if everyone is required to contribute or if they are free to bring their own supplies to group workings instead.

5. Find a way to keep a record of who contributes what and how the supplies are used. This can save you a lot of grief in the long run if someone questions how the group resources are being used.

DESIGNING GROUP RITUALS

A magical ritual is a ceremony performed by two or more people with a shared intent to raise and direct magical power. They can be performed for a variety of purposes. Group rituals can be as complex or as simple as you and your fellow magical practitioners choose to make them. Many different magical traditions use rituals, and they vary greatly from tradition to tradition.

Though they can take quite a bit more preparation than even the most complex individual spells, and a great deal of coordination with your fellow practitioners, rituals are powerful tools that will help you accomplish your magical goals.

Deciding to raise and direct energy in a setting with clear boundaries and goals allows you to amplify your magical power. Rituals are a useful framework that a group can share to clarify what is going on and assist in the coordination of their magical efforts.

Though this book focuses on wealth magic, rituals can be designed for a variety of purposes, including celebrating a season or accomplishment, harnessing the power of the full moon or fostering spiritual growth (to name just a few)!

This section assumes that everyone can participate in the ritual in person. There is a section at the end that discusses adapting this approach to virtual settings.

Tips for making your ritual a success

1. Take the time to carefully plan your ritual. If possible, make this a communal process. If your fellow magical practitioners are involved in the planning process, they will be much more likely to understand and integrate the concepts underlying symbolic and magical choices.
2. Clearly define the roles and responsibilities for each participant. Make sure everyone understands what they need to do. Do they need to wear

clothes of a certain colour? Do parts need to be memorized or can they be read? Do participants need to bring anything with them?

3. If you plan to have attendees at your ritual, make sure they know what to do. Even if someone is not taking an active role in the ritual itself, they need to know what their responsibilities will be. Does a participant need to remain silent throughout? Do they need to repeat any words? Who will guide them? Reserve some time before the ritual starts to share this information.

4. Remind participants and attendees that though the ritual itself is a group event, each person will have to process what they experience during the ritual and after. Encourage people to journal and reflect on what develops. The real magic begins once the ritual concludes.

Physical environment and safety

For a ritual to be a success, the participants and attendees must feel safe and welcome. When you choose the place to conduct the ritual, take these elements into consideration:

- The space should be accessible to all attendees and participants.
- Make sure you have seating arrangements for people who can't stand throughout the entire ritual.
- If you choose to conduct the ritual outdoors, make a contingency plan for bad weather (will the ritual be rescheduled or moved indoors?).
- Is the location safe? Don't plan to use property that isn't yours or a location that might put your participants at risk (for example, a public place where people who don't understand your good intentions might get a glimpse of what is going on).
- Have a good first-aid kit on hand. Rituals often involve things like moving around in the dark, lighting candles and other activities that could result in painful mishaps. A first-aid kit is a must.

Group and personal intentions

Most rituals focus on a particular group intention. It might be a ritual for the benefit of one person (let's get Ted the start-up cash they need for their new business), or it could be for the benefit of all (let's channel the energy of the full moon to manifest constant prosperity in our lives). Sometimes the group will only focus on that one intention. But at other times, you can invite individual participants and attendees to set their own intentions so that the magical power raised also goes toward individual goals. When you are starting out, I'd suggest sticking with one group goal until you get used to the process.

Make these decisions first

1. Choose the primary intent/purpose for the ritual.
2. Decide the general structure of your ritual. Do you want to cast a ritual circle? Do you want to process into the location and do your work outside a circle?
3. Pick the time and location. Consider indoor and outdoor spots.
4. Do you want to call on the assistance of any spiritual allies such as gods, goddesses, ancestors or angels? If so, it is important to build a relationship with whomever you are going to ask for assistance prior to inviting them into your ritual space.
5. Approximately how many people are going to actively participate? (So you can make sure there are enough roles to go around.)

Make these decisions next

1. Choose which ritual components you want to include (see list of potential components below).
2. Decide how you want to enact each component. For example, if you want to cast a circle, how will it be cast? Will someone walk the boundary of the ritual space? Will they simply visualize a circle being drawn or will they speak words, sprinkle blessed water or use some other method to cast the circle?

3. Figure out who will perform each piece of the ritual. Also consider assigning responsibility for writing each part. Will the person performing the part also write it if there are words to speak or actions to take? Or will someone be responsible for creating the entire thing? Note: When assigning parts, don't forget to specify who will be overseeing the ritual as a whole. You can call them the high priest or priestess; you can call them the ringmaster or head honcho or even the big cheese. But make sure that someone will be in charge of administering the ritual. By that, I mean making sure everyone is there when the ritual starts, ensuring all the supplies are present before the ritual starts, and announcing, "Hey folks, we really are getting started now, settle down!" If you are administering the ritual, do your best not to let the power go to your head. If you aren't administering the ritual, do your best to listen to your ritual runner and not drive them mad. Remember that if you continue to work with the same group, it's likely that you will eventually take the opposite role, and people have long memories. Be nice!

Make some notes

While you are making the decisions above, jot down notes so you can remember everything that you or the group have decided. If the whole group is participating in planning, the note-taker should confirm the decisions as they are made. "Steve says he is willing to cast the circle and will write a simple chant for that part – I'm going to write that down, unless there are any changes."

Keep track of:

- What ritual components will be included
- Who will be doing what
- What materials and supplies will be needed
- Who will be responsible for bringing what

POTENTIAL RITUAL COMPONENTS

Here is a list of actions and activities you may wish to include in a ritual. This list is just a suggestion, and you and your group may come up with many more ideas!

- **Individual preparation** – Often taking place before the formal part of the ritual starts, this could include things like leading the group in a grounding and centring exercise, smudging attendees with incense, or spiritually cleansing attendees with blessed water or oils. Each participant could do this for themselves, or one person could lead the group.

- **Opening/casting a circle** – Whether you are casting a circle or not, something needs to symbolically mark the start of the ritual itself. This could be a song, a chant or a ritual greeting that all attendees exchange. If a circle is cast, it could be visualized by the group or physically cast by sprinkling water or making a physical mark on the ground. Circles are useful for containing magical power until it is ready to be released.

- **Inviting entities to help with the magical work or join in the celebration** – If you work with a diverse group, this can be an interesting and informative part of your ritual. You can invite each participant to verbally welcome in whomever they feel would be willing to help with the intent of the ritual (a personal guide, patron god or saint). Or one person can be in charge of inviting entities that the group has chosen beforehand. This is usually done with a verbal chant or call but can also be done with drumming or singing.

- **Stating the intent** – Once physical and non-physical attendees are all present, it is a good idea to clearly and explicitly state the intent of the ritual, so everyone is working toward the same goal. If individual goals are a part of the ritual, they can be stated after the primary intent has been declared.

- **Creative expression** – This is a part of ritual that I love, and I wish there was more of it! This could include a short play aligned with the purpose of the ritual, a recitation of a poem, singing, drawing or dancing.

Again, specific participants could be chosen to prepare something, or the group could work on a spontaneous collage to support the purpose of the ritual (if something like this is planned, make sure to have all needed supplies in the ritual area before the circle is cast!).

- **Raising magical power** – There are countless ways to raise magical power, from drumming, clapping hands and chanting to meditation, dancing and humming. Choose something that the group feels comfortable with. Remember that people should be visualizing the intent of the ritual while raising power, so don't choose a complex dance or something that will make it difficult to focus.

- **Releasing magical power** – A key part of the ritual is knowing when to release all that wonderful power that has been raised by the group. I suggest that one person is designated to release the power by shouting, ringing a bell or some other easily identified signal. This can be a challenging part of managing group energy. Pick the person who is most comfortable with sensing energy.

- **Saying farewell to any entities invited to join the ritual** – If you choose to welcome any non-physical entities into the ritual space to help with your magical work, it is important to thank them and say farewell to them after the work is over. First, it is only polite. Second, it lets them know that their attentions can be directed elsewhere. Sometimes this part of a ritual is called "banishing", which some folks find too harsh a word. Depending on the entities involved, decide how you want to say goodbye to those that have helped you. Something as simple as "Thank you, spirits, for joining us, our work is completed, and you may be on your way" is enough.

- **Closing/uncasting the circle** – If you chose to cast a circle, please uncast it when you are done. Only rarely should a circle remain after a ritual is complete (for example, if it is performed in a group's dedicated ritual space). In most cases, the circle should be uncast so any remaining magical power may dissipate.

- **Grounding excess energy** – After all that work, participants may feel super-energized and perhaps even a little ungrounded. Raising magical

THE GOLDEN GRIMOIRE

power can make you feel that way. Individuals or the group as a whole may wish to spend time grounding out that excess energy. I often do this by lying flat on the ground or floor and visualizing all the excess draining out of me and soaking into the earth. It's simple, and it works.

- **Post-ritual discussion** – Everyone just went through a powerful and exciting experience! So now it's time to talk about it. This serves both a practical and a magical purpose. On a practical level, the group can discuss what did and didn't work well, especially if you decided to try something new. On a spiritual and magical level, this is the time for people to share their personal experiences during the ritual, which can be the first step to integrating the ritual and its results into their mundane and magical lives.

THE GOLDEN GRIMOIRE

APPENDIX: SPELL PREPARATION AND CONCLUSION TECHNIQUES

PREPARING YOURSELF

Sometimes you will feel exceptionally in tune with yourself when preparing to work some magic. You'll be in a state of flow, and you will already feel connected to the universe in indescribable ways. There will be other times when stress, daily worries or even minor fatigue will make you feel a bit off. Or your personal energy field may be too erratic to allow you to concentrate. At those times, you can turn to grounding and centring techniques to prepare yourself for magical work.

Even when you feel fine, pausing for a few moments to ground and centre will let your subconscious mind and your intuition know that you are about to do something special.

Grounding

Grounding is important because it helps you feel stable and calm. It balances your energy and allows you to be aware of the present moment. Grounding connects you with the solid and supportive energy of the earth so you can even out your personal power and prepare for magic. There are many different ways to ground yourself, so you will need to experiment with different approaches to find the ones that work best for you. Here are several you can try.

- **Breathing** – Taking deep, slow breaths calms and balances your energy and helps you to relax. If you need a little more structure in your breathing exercises, try fourfold breathing. Breathe in for a count of four, hold your breath for a count of four, breathe out for a count of four, then hold the exhale for a count of four. Start out by trying five cycles and then expand to ten if it feels like the method is working for you.

- **Connecting to the earth** – A simple way to ground yourself: get outside, take your shoes off and walk around barefoot. Allow the stabilizing power of the earth to infuse your body with its influences. You can also try sitting or lying on the ground if that appeals to you.
- **Crystals** – If you can't get outside, you can rely on a favourite crystal or stone to help you ground. Smoky quartz, obsidian and other dark-coloured stones work great. Or you might want to try working with a stone from one of your favourite places. Hold it in the hand you don't write with. Focus on the feeling of it in your hand. Picture its calming influence infusing your body.
- **Gardening or tending plants** – Similar to connecting with the earth, spending some time in your home garden or tending your favourite potted plants can help you feel more connected and at peace. Of course, you may find yourself getting lost in your gardening, so do this when you have ample time to enjoy your plants!
- **Mindfulness** – A simple yet deceptively powerful approach, mindfulness can bring you calm and feelings of connection at any time. Close your eyes and focus on what your body feels. Then open your eyes and spend a few minutes genuinely looking at your surroundings and what is going on around you. Don't pass judgement on what you see or experience, just let the information flow through you. Observe the present moment.
- **Spending time with pets** – If you have a pet, spending time with them likely lowers your blood pressure. But doing so can also settle your personal energy field and help you get ready. Spend some time cuddling with an animal you love, and you'll be ready to cast your spell in no time.
- **Stretching** – Whether taking an organized approach, such as doing formal yoga poses, or simply identifying the stiff areas of your body and giving them a good stretch, doing so can ground your energy and help you focus on the here and now, preparing you for magic.
- **Visualizations** – If you picture what you'd like to accomplish, you

can make it happen. Visualization helps direct energy to accomplish your goals. Close your eyes, take a few deep breaths and visualize roots growing out of the bottom of your feet and twining deep into the earth. Feel your energy equalize. Or picture a beam of pure energy emanating from the centre of the earth, shining up to and through your heart and disappearing into the heavens. Feel the calming, balancing effects of the beam. There are countless other visualizations you can experiment with.

- **Walking** – Taking a quiet stroll in a place you love is a great way to reset yourself and manage your energy. Though an outside location might be the first place that springs to mind, you might want to try walking around a beloved shopping centre, a library or another indoor location that relaxes you and evens out your energy.

Centring

Centring helps focus your mind and dismiss any distractions before you start your magical work. Some of the grounding techniques listed above double as centring techniques. This means that if you ground, you may not feel the need to centre yourself afterwards. But if you do feel the need to refocus your attention, try one of these methods.

- **Body scan** – Focusing on physical sensations in your body can help you push away mental distractions. Start at your feet and focus on how they feel. Wiggle your toes and experience the sensation of movement. Move up to your ankles and place your consciousness there. Continue to move your attention up your body until you have visited every part, ending with the top of your head. You'll be tuned into yourself and ready to get to work!

- **Chanting** – A repetitive chant of one word or a short phrase can help focus your attention and draw yourself inwards. It could be something as simple as repeating, "Calm and centred" over and over again. Allow the rhythm of the words and the sound of your voice to bring you to a state of calm and clarity.

- **Sound** – Sound vibrations are wonderful tools for centring. Bells, triangles, tuning forks and singing bowls can all be used to focus your attention. You might need to experiment with which sound frequencies work best for you, or you could already have something at home that does a wonderful job at bringing your consciousness to the here and now.

- **Visualizations** – Just like the visualizations for grounding above, there are many different images you can experiment with. When I perform centring visualizations, I focus on my heart because I feel it's a good symbol of the centre of not only my body but also my being. Try picturing a small gold ball manifesting in the centre of your heart. Picture a beautiful golden thread emanating from the ball. See a crystal pendulum weight attach itself to the end of the thread. Set the pendulum swinging and feel it anchor you to your current place and time.

PREPARING YOUR MAGICAL TOOLS

There are two different ways to approach magical tools. Eventually, you'll decide how you want to treat the ones you work with. You can either have dedicated tools that you only use for magic, or you might use items around your house that you also use for other purposes (like using a wooden spoon to make your pasta and as a magic wand).

The nice thing about using general-use items is that there are a variety of them all around your home. With a little creativity, you can turn almost any item into a magical tool. This really helps when you are first starting out, or when you need to work a spell quickly and don't have the time to go shopping. One danger of doing this is that occasionally the general-use item attains a special status in your mind and then you are incapable of using it for anything but magic anyway! So choose cautiously.

Dedicated items that are purchased and only used for magical work accrue power and important associations over time. Seeking out and selecting a dedicated magical tool can be a significant step in magical workings. Because they are carefully stored away from mundane items, they don't have to be repeatedly cleansed or prepared. However, if you decide to work only with dedicated tools, you might feel limited when you are first starting out.

I work with a variety of tools. Some are dedicated solely for magical use. Others are items that I use for other purposes. You can easily incorporate both types of tool into your magical practice.

Dedicated tools

If you wish to prepare a dedicated magical tool for use, you might consider some of the following steps.

- **Physically and spiritually cleansing the item** – When you first purchase your tool, physically clean it of any dust, dirt or grime. Then clean it spiritually. This banishes any influences that the item may have picked up before it got to you. Cleansing methods include rinsing it under running water, passing it through incense smoke, burying it or covering it in salt, or leaving it in the light of the moon or the Sun. Please think carefully and choose a spiritual cleansing method that won't hurt the item. (For example, candles shouldn't be cleansed in the light of the Sun.)

- **Personalizing the item** – Even if you have purchased the item, do something to it to make it uniquely yours. You can make this as complex as you'd like. For example, you could paint or carve your initial or a special magical symbol on it. Or you could wrap part of it in thread or ribbon in an important symbolic colour.

- **Dedicating the item** – Conduct a miniature ritual in which you formally dedicate the item to your magical work. This doesn't have to be fancy. Light a candle of an appropriate colour. State what you'll be using the tool for and what you want it to help you accomplish. Ask any entities you work with to bless the tool.

- **Storing the item** – If your tool will only be used for magical purposes, make sure you have a safe place to store it. It should be a place that only you have access to, to avoid someone else touching it or unintentionally using it for a mundane purpose. (Exception: If you work magic with someone and you don't mind them using your tools, you can store them in a communal space.)

PREPARING YOUR WORKSPACE

Depending on the spell and on your personal situation, you could be working magic anywhere: at a dedicated altar, sitting on your bed, at your dining room table or out in the woods. Just like choosing magical tools, selecting a location is an extremely personal thing. In general, you should prepare your working space as much as needed to make yourself feel comfortable. If that means you empty out an entire room, clean it from top to bottom and then spend days spiritually cleansing it, then that is what you should do. (Just the idea exhausts me, to be honest!) If it means you feel cosy sitting on your couch with a rose-scented tealight burning and using your coffee table as your altar, then do that! Here are some things you can consider while deciding how you want to prepare your magical workspace.

- **Physical and spiritual cleansing** – Decluttering, tidying and physically cleaning a space can help free up its energy and make it available for use. So consider putting things away and generally sprucing things up before getting to work. Likewise, you can light a white candle and burn some sandalwood incense to spiritually cleanse the place before you start. Or you can sprinkle some salt or blessed water around to prepare your space for magic.

- **Lighting** – Natural light is lovely if available. If not, consider candles (traditional or LED), lamps and lanterns, or other forms of mood lighting. It's also perfectly okay to use the room's standard lighting, particularly if you are doing something like building a tool or creating a talisman.

- **Sound and music** – Music moves the soul. The soundscape you create during spell work can contribute a great deal to your magic. Relaxing or atmospheric music is a must for me when I start my work. If you are planning on streaming music, make sure that your playlist won't be interrupted by commercials because they can jar you out of your carefully crafted state of mind. If I am working magic by myself, I often use noise-cancelling headphones to block out the distractions of the world while I work.

- **Decorations** – Just like sound, our surroundings influence our state of mind and therefore how well we can focus on our magical work. Some folks prefer a clean and clear workspace. Others like to decorate with crystals, statues, symbols and cloths. Play around to find out what you like.

- **Scents** – Incense, scented oils and scented candles can greatly influence our mood. Scents also have important magical correspondences. If you wish to scent the air of your magical workspace, make sure to choose something that complements your magical intent. Also, no matter how perfectly a scent matches your intent, do not use it if you hate it or if you are allergic to it! That will be far too distracting and will end up working against you.

- **Gathering your tools** – As part of preparing your workspace, gather all your materials before you get started. Stopping to hunt for a pair of scissors, a candleholder or the image of one of your non-physical allies can cause frustration and ruin your focus. Check and double-check to make sure you have what you need. Write it all down if you have to. Picture yourself going through the steps of your spell so you don't leave anything out. If your spell requires a candle, do you have something to light it with? If it requires water, do you have a cup of water on hand? Be thorough!

- **Beverages** – This may sound like a silly item but hear me out. In many of the spells in this book, you are doing a lot of reflecting or thinking. In others you are constructing tools. In both of these cases, having something to drink on hand can keep you feeling relaxed and happy while you work. Clear water, refreshing juice, or a cosy cup of coffee or tea can help sustain your efforts. Bonus points if you flavour your drink to match your intentions!

THE GOLDEN GRIMOIRE

CONCLUDING YOUR WORK

When you finish a spell, you are likely to end up with some used magical materials. There are several different ways to go about disposing of these remnants. This is what I like to do.

- **Items that I want to use again (candleholders, bowls, plates, etc.)** – I remove any remaining material that needs to be disposed of (old wax, ashes, pieces of paper, etc.). I gently physically clean the item, if possible. I like to use warm soapy water to do it, if the item can stand it. After physically cleansing the item, I spiritually cleanse it with salt or by wafting incense over it. Then I put the item away where it belongs (either in my magical toolkit or wherever else it lives).
- **Magical tools (wands, skewers, cups, etc.)** – I wrap them in a black cloth and store them with my magical supplies.
- **Items to dispose of (wax remnants, incense ash, paper, etc.)** – I fold these up in white paper and respectfully dispose of them in the trash. If it is something I know won't hurt the environment, like ashes from plain burned paper, I might give the item back to the earth by letting the wind carry it away or burying it. But there are so many times I am not sure of the components of the wax or other materials I use, that I don't want to leave it up to chance. So generally I throw my old components in the trash.

One final note:

To ensure success, once you have performed the magical work, you must follow up by doing the mundane work. If you work a spell to find a job, search for and apply for jobs. Don't just sit around and wait for one to fall into your lap. Give the universe opportunities to respond to your magic!

ACKNOWLEDGEMENTS

Thank you to my agent and all the folks at Watkins who helped make this book a reality.

A huge thanks to all the members of the Black Candle Coven past and present (you know who you are) for listening, giving feedback and generally being the best of humans.

Extra thanks to Pam, for providing emotional support, sympathy and cute dogs during times of emotional distress.

As always, thanks to Molly, my sister in crime in all things.

And thanks to Paige, for your constant encouragement.

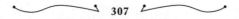

INDEX

Note: page numbers in **bold** refer to illustrations.

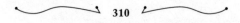

THE GOLDEN GRIMOIRE

THE GOLDEN GRIMOIRE

INDEX

The manufacturer's authorised representative
in the EU for product safety is:

Eucomply OÜ

Pärnu mnt 139b-14, 11317 Tallinn, Estonia

hello@eucompliancepartner.com

www.eucompliancepartner.com